WIT & WISDOM of FISHING

CONTRIBUTING WRITERS

LOUIS BIGNAMI

ROBERT JONES

WILLIAM R. (BILL) ROONEY

JOEL VANCE

PUBLICATIONS INTERNATIONAL, LTD.

Contributing Writers

Louis Bignami is the author of more than three dozen books on travel and the outdoors. A full-time writer since 1969, he has sold more than 10,000 books and columns nationally and internationally. He is a member of the Outdoor Writers Association of America, as well as other professional organizations.

Robert Jones, winner of the Outdoor Writers of Canada 1996 Award for Excellence in Outdoor Writing, is a columnist for *BC Outdoors* and *Real Outdoors* magazines. He has contributed to *Ontario Out of Doors, Canadian Fishing Annual,* and other publications and is the author of numerous books and magazine articles.

William R. (Bill) Rooney has three decades of experience as a writer and editor, serving on the staffs of *Outdoor Life* and *American Forests* magazines. His articles have appeared in major national outdoor publications, as well as the *Washington Post, Ford Times,* and elsewhere. He is a long-time member of the Outdoor Writers Association of America.

Joel Vance spent more than 20 years as an award-winning news and magazine writer for the Missouri Department of Conservation before becoming a full-time freelance writer. He is the author of four books and is an Excellence in Craft honoree by the Outdoor Writers Association of America, which also awarded him its top conservation honor.

Cover Illustration: Dan Krovatin

Illustrations: Dan Krovatin, C.B. Mordan

Acknowledgments

Publications International, Ltd., has made every effort to locate the owners of all copyrighted material to obtain permission to use the selections that appear in this book. Any errors or omissions are unintentional; corrections, if necessary will be made in future editions.

Page 12: Copyright 1994 by Grant McClintock and Mike Crockett. Reprinted from *Flywater* with permission of Lyons & Burford, Publishers.

Pages 13, 54, 59, 91: From *Anatomy of a Fisherman* by Robert Traver (John Voelker) by permission of Grace Voelker.

Pages 14, 33, 95, 126-7, 141: From *The Old Man and The Boy* by Robert Ruarke, Copyright 1953, 1954, 1955, 1956, 1957 by Robert C. Ruark and Renewed in 1981 by Harold Matson, Paul Gitlin and Chemical Bank. *The Old Man's Boy Grows Older* by Robert Ruarke, Copyright 1957, 1958, 1959, 1960, 1961 by Robert Ruark and Renewed in 1981 by Harold Matson, Paul Gitlin and Chemical Bank. Reprinted by permission of Henry Holt & Co., Inc.

Pages 26, 126: Excerpts by Lee Wulff with permission of Joan Wulff. First published in *Outdoor Life* in 1983, and again in 1991.

Pages 25, 31, 55, 73, 77, 99, 107, 113, 159, 169: Excerpts from *Darwin's Bass* by Paul Quinnett courtesy of Keokee Co. Publishing.

Page 29: Excerpt by Ted Trueblood courtesy of Jack Trueblood.

Pages 57, 89, 93, 99, 135, 145: Excerpts courtesy of *Field & Stream* Magazine.

Page 69: Excerpt from *Of Bows & Trolls & Scaly Things* by Lionel Atwill courtesy of the author.

Pages 71, 77, 79, 81, 84, 133, 155: Excerpts from *Tap's Tips* by H.G. Tapply courtesy of the author.

Page 86: From "Trout Fishing in Europe." Reprinted with permission of Scribner, a Division of Simon & Schuster, from *By-Line: Ernest Hemingway*, edited by William White. Copyright 1967 by Mary Hemingway.

Page 101: From "Big Two-Hearted River: Part I." Reprinted with permission of Scribner, a Division of Simon & Schuster, from *The Complete Short Stories of Ernest Hemingway*. Copyright 1925 Charles Scribner's Sons. Copyright renewed 1953 by Ernest Hemingway.

Page 112: Excerpt by Norman Strung by permission of Sil Strung.

Page 129: Excerpt from *You Can Always Tell a Fisherman* by Corey Ford courtesy of the Trustees of Dartmouth College.

Page 169: From *A Sand County Almanac* by Aldo Leopold. Copyright 1966 by Aldo Leopold. Used by permission of University of Oxford Press, Inc.

Page 170: Excerpt from *Take a Grownup Fishing* by Gene Hill courtesy of the author.

Louis Weber, C.E.O.
Publications International, Ltd.
7373 North Cicero Avenue
Lincolnwood, Illinois 60646

Permission is never granted for commercial purposes.

Manufactured in U.S.A.

8 7 6 5 4 3 2 1

ISBN: 0-7853-2194-2

Library of Congress Catalog Card Number: 96-72657

CONTENTS

INTRODUCTION ⌇ 6

OLD ANGLER'S WISDOM ⌇ 8
Ernest Hemingway, Herbert Hoover, and other "old-timers"
offer up some grandfatherly advice and fishin' philosophy.

FISHING MEMORIES ⌇ 26
It's the small moments that make this sport magical.
These reflections should help you remember why you
first picked up that old fishing pole.

THE ONE THAT GOT AWAY ⌇ 48
Sit back and listen to some of the biggest whoppers and fish
stories since your last fishing trip with cousin Ernie.

FISHING LESSONS ⌇ 67
Our angling experts divulge some tried-and-true tips and
secrets that may even have you reeling in the big one.

TRUE STORIES ⌇ 86
From puzzled presidents to gigantic pike, discover some
incredible-but-true tales from the world of angling.

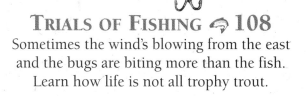

TRIALS OF FISHING ☞ 108

Sometimes the wind's blowing from the east
and the bugs are biting more than the fish.
Learn how life is not all trophy trout.

THE LIGHTER SIDE OF FISHING ☞ 129

You'll laugh along with these amusing quotes and tales in
praise of seasickness, worms, and other angling delights
from the likes of Mark Twain and Isaak Walton.

HOOKS, LINES & SINKERS ☞ 150

Like great poetry, great fishing can inspire the pen to paper.
Find out what Shakespeare, Wordsworth, and others have
had to say about the "gentle art."

FISHY FACTS ☞ 170

Discover world-record fish, handy hints, and angling
oddities with this collection of fishing trivia.

INTRODUCTION

AN ACQUAINTANCE sneers that he hates it when he is forced to "commit fishing." I've watched him flail at the water with a fly rod as if he were fighting off yellowjackets and can understand that for him fishing is far less entertaining than it is for those of us who watch him do it. But for the 60 million Americans who regularly and joyfully commit fishing, it is not only entertainment, it is relief and release from everyday cares, it is a source of healthy and tasty food, and for many it is a consuming passion that transcends mere hobby.

Fishing is, after all, an essential part of our culture. Fish stories are legendary. When you accuse someone of telling a whopper, you aren't talking about hamburgers—you're referring to a fish lie . . . er, story. And look at all the fishing lingo that has pervaded our language. You fish for compliments. You try not to be a cold fish, and sometimes you have to fish or cut bait. Just don't carp about it.

Once I was fly fishing without a shirt and a popping bug embedded itself in the skin over my breastbone. I had read that if you loop a piece of string around the bend of the hook, press the hook eye down, then jerk up on the string, the hook will pop free without doing any damage. Since the hook was hidden by my chin, I stood in front of a mirror with a piece of string, ready to use this bit of fishing wisdom. But everything is backward in a mirror. I was totally disoriented and started laughing. Maybe it wasn't "wit," but it certainly was low humor and that's the next best thing. Wit and wisdom of fishing? Commit fishing long enough and you'll fill a treasure chest of memories with both.

That's why this book is so much fun. We can find ourselves here, or maybe learn something new, or get a laugh over someone else's fishing problems. Find out who was our "fishingest president" (and which presidents didn't fare so well with hook and line). All anglers are equal under the water. A fish neither knows nor cares who is on the other end of the line and a president has just as much (or as little) chance of landing a trophy as does the kid with the cane pole and wriggling worm.

In the heat of summer, I always visit a nearby catfish pond, heave a chunk of turkey liver into the deep part of the pond, lay back in the shade on soft grass with a good book, and subconsciously hope that no fish disturbs my reading by molesting the liver. Reading is almost as much fun as fishing . . . and reading about fishing is almost too much fun for anyone. You have a rare treat in the pages ahead.

Just try not to get the pages stuck together with catfish slime or dried bits of liver. . . .

—JOEL VANCE

OLD ANGLER'S WISDOM

"ALL GOOD FISHERMEN stay young until they die, for fishing is the only dream of youth that doth not grow stale with age."

—J.W. MULLER

MY MENTOR

I WAS 14 when I started wielding a fly rod, and did fairly
well that first summer. However, when fall weather chilled
the river my expertise plummeted with the mercury, and I
reverted to using worms. I was thus engaged when "Old
Will" appeared. He was only in his late fifties, but they had
been hard, hell-raising years
interrupted by two wars.
When he saw the worm
on my hook I got a
proper dressing down, then
he demonstrated that trout
would, indeed, still take flies.

He was a graceful, accurate caster with river smarts most
anglers could only dream of attaining. Within seconds a
rainbow danced across the rapids. After releasing two more
fish he waded ashore, then from a small enamelled box
plucked a fly he identified only as a "brown bug." It had a
spindly, brown body, with long, skimpy hackles. "When ya
git home," he growled, "git yerself some gunny sack and
some brown feathers outta yer pillow, and make yer own."

He pointed to a rock in the river. "Git downstream from
where ya figger the fish is layin', then study yer water
upstream. Ya gotta chuck yer fly in jest the right spot, so's
it'll wash down like a real bug. Keep yer line slack, 'cause if
the fly drags, the trout knows it ain't the Real McCoy. If yer
line looks like it's gonna drag, flip it upstream a bit. Now

chuck that fly up above that rock and let it come back on a slack line like I told ya. When a fish grabs it, the line'll give a little twitch—and ya hit jest like a rattlesnake bitin' a baby bunny. But ya gotta pay attention or ya won't see nuthin'."

I cast where Old Will had pointed, then, without seeing the fish hit or setting the hook, I was promptly into a plump rainbow.

"By God, boy, ya learn fast!" crowed my mentor. "Always knew I missed my callin'—I shoulda bin a teacher."

Old Will has long since passed on; however, whenever using nymphs I first "read" the water, then pick the best position from which to cast. And if I neglect mending the line, I hear a gravel voice growl, "Flip that line up and git some slack in 'er. Ya fly fishin' or tryin' ta snag 'em?" Lessons properly taught are never forgotten, so maybe Old Will really did miss his calling.

"No HUMAN being, however great,
or powerful, was ever so free as a fish."

—JOHN RUSKIN, THE TWO PATHS

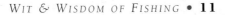

WORDS OF WISDOM

WHEN I ASKED a sprightly angler in his mid-80s what period of the day he considered best for fishing, Mike sat back in his chair and puffed reflectively on his pipe for a few moments, pondering my question. "Well," he answered, "I'd say early mornin's and evenin's are best, and that's for sure." Then he lowered his head slightly and peered at me over the top of his spectacles. "But all the hours in between 'em both are just as good."

"THE GODS DO not deduct from man's allotted span the hours spent in fishing."

—*BABYLONIAN PROVERB, OFTEN QUOTED BY HERBERT HOOVER*

"THERE IS AN OLD saying that one can never enter the same river twice. The river is always new; the man is forever changed."

—*MIKE CROCKETT AND GRANT McCLINTOCK, FLYWATER*

"NO MAN IS BORN an Artist nor an Angler."

—*IZAAK WALTON, THE COMPLEAT ANGLER*

"THE PLEASANT'ST ANGLING is to see the fish
Cut with her golden oars the silver stream,
And greedily devour the treacherous bait."

—WILLIAM SHAKESPEARE, MUCH ADO ABOUT NOTHING

"TO LIVE is not necessary. To fish is necessary."

—LATIN INSCRIPTION

"WITHIN THE pool's abysmal dun
A salmon eyes the shattered sun:
Salmon and water move as one."

—WILLIAM JEFFREY

"THE TRUTH IS that trout fishermen scheme
and lie and toss in their sleep. They dream of great dripping
trout, shapely and elusive as mermaids, and arise cranky
and haggard from their fantasies. They are moody and
neglectful and all of them a little daft. Moreover they are
inclined to drink too much."

—ROBERT TRAVER, ANATOMY OF A FISHERMAN

FISHING OR HUNTING?

WHILE MANY anglers claim they do not hunt, I beg to differ. Fishing *is* hunting, no doubt about it.

The angler is the hunter and the fish, no matter whether a six-inch bluegill or a 20-foot great white shark, is the hunted. When a fish bites, setting the hook is as much an attack on your quarry as pulling a trigger or loosing an arrow.

However, whereas a well-placed, killing shot is the culmination of a successful hunt, hooking a fish merely sets the stage for the next of several steps: fighting, landing or boating it, then—if you wish—releasing it. There is always an opportunity to show mercy and respect, like two great warriors who have shared a battle and may someday meet again. The last step is the crucial difference between hunting and fishing.

"THE WHOLE PURPOSE of summer fishing,' the Old Man said, 'is not to worry about catching fish, but to just get out of the house and set and think a little. Also, the womenfolk are very bad-tempered in the summer. The less you hang around the premises the less trouble you're apt to get in.'"

—*ROBERT RUARK*, THE OLD MAN AND THE BOY

"It is the birds and other creatures peculiar to the water that render fly-fishing so pleasant; were they all destroyed, and nothing left but the mere fish, one might as well stand and fish in a stone cattle-trough."

—*Richard Jefferies*, The Life of the Fields

"Time is but the stream I go a-fishing in. I drink at it; but while I drink I see the sandy bottom and detect how shallow it is. Its thin current slides away, but eternity remains. I would drink deeper; fish in the sky, where the bottom is pebbly with stars."

—Henry David Thoreau

ADD IT UP

THE BASIC EQUATION for "consistent" fishing success is always the same: location + timing + knowledge = fish. "Consistent" is stressed to remove "luck" from this equation, for luck is inconsistent and undependable—just ask legions of lottery players.

"Location" and "timing" mean being in the right place at the right time, but "knowledge" is difficult to define. There are various levels, and many things about which to be knowledgeable—like knowing when to be in the right place at the right time. Anglers read magazines and books on the topic; ask questions of anglers who are already experienced and successful; attend courses aimed at specific fishing techniques; and watch videos—even an occasional television program that doesn't insult a viewer's intelligence. They learn about spawning cycles, migration patterns, habitat and temperature preferences, entomology, and food chains. They acquire topographical maps and marine charts to study, marking down known or potentially productive areas and the best routes to reach them. By learning the limitations of their rod, reel, line, leader, and hooks, they can use their tackle effectively on occasions when larger than average fish are encountered.

There are many different ways of following this simple equation, but they all add up to angling success.

"RAINBOW TROUT fishing is as different
from brook fishing as prize fighting is from boxing."

—ERNEST HEMINGWAY

"THERE WERE LOTS of people who committed
crimes during the year who would not have done
so if they had been fishing, and I assure you
that the increase in crime is due to a lack of those
qualities of mind and character which impregnate the
soul of every fisherman except those who get no bites."

—HERBERT HOOVER

"TO LOOK into the depths of the sea
is to behold the imagination of the Unknown."

—VICTOR HUGO

FEEDING FRENZY

WHILE STROLLING ALONG the shoreline of a stocked trout pond, I overheard two elderly anglers discussing their day's catch. One revealed he had caught three pan-sized rainbows that afternoon, all on corn kernels. "Yesterday all they'd take was miniature marshmallows," he said. "Day before, it was cheddar cheese or nothing. I can't believe how fussy they get."

"I know," his friend replied. "Kinda makes you wonder if they're coming from a hatchery or a delicatessen, don't it?"

"For sure. You know, I ain't used a worm yet this spring."

"Hah!" his partner cackled, "You're turnin' into a real purist!"

"**F**ISH DINNERS WILL make a man spring like a flea."

—*THOMAS JORDAN*

"**H**OWEVER BAD the sport, it keeps you young, or makes you young again, and you need not follow Ponce de Leon to the western wilderness, when, in any river you knew of yore, you can find the fountain of youth."

—*ANDREW LANG*

"CAN THE FISH love the fisherman?"

—MARTIAL, EPIGRAMS

"A SKILLFUL Angler ought to be a general scholar, and seen
in all the liberal sciences, as a Grammarian, to know
how either to write or discourse on his Art in true terms,
either without affection or rudeness."

—GERVASE MARKHAM

"THE ARTIFICIAL BREEDING of domestic fish . . .
is apparently destined to occupy an extremely conspicuous
place in the history of man's efforts to compensate his
prodigal waste of the gifts of nature."

—GEORGE PERKINS MARSH

BOYS WILL BE BOYS

THE BOYS, perhaps eight or ten years old, perch on a rocky outcropping bordering a slow-moving backwater—a perfect place to practice their budding angling skills. Their tackle is basic: a length of monofilament line wrapped around a piece of scrap lumber notched at both ends, a sinker, hook, and worms for bait.

Elbows resting on the bridge railing, I watch as their patience is rewarded with a yellow perch about 10 inches long—large enough to please any angler. The other boy adjusts the depth of his hook and promptly nabs his own perch. Four more follow, each whacked energetically on the head with a small piece of driftwood, then placed in a shaded rock crevice for safekeeping.

I am about to leave when one boy hooks something larger. After a hectic tug of war, a walleye is hauled onto the rock shelf, then frantically kicked well away from the water's edge. The golden-hued beauty—maybe three pounds—is laid to rest with the perch.

Just as the boys start fishing again, a boat rounds the corner and cruises upstream toward them. Low profile, raised casting platforms fore and aft, swivelling pedestal seats, bow-mounted electric motor, and lots of little black boxes to divulge underwater terrain, presence of fish, oxygen content, temperature, and who knows what else. The two middle-aged men have a half dozen rods and reels rigged and ready for use, as well as oversized tackle boxes that are probably filled to capacity. "Having any luck?" asks the man in the bow.

"Purdy good," the boys answer in unison. They scramble to the crevice and hold up their catch. The men are impressed and compliment the boys' angling skills. Then they lower the electric motor and back well off to probe the river with bottom-bouncing jigs. They are gentlemen, for their lures never infringe on the boys' territory.

The walleye remain cooperative and everyone catches fish before their feeding spree ends. One each for the boys, two each for the boaters. After a few minutes spent cruising slowly around the area, searching, the men start the outboard, wish the youngsters luck, then continue upstream.

From my vantage point I see the longing in the boys' eyes for that beautiful boat and the expensive tackle, and the thoughtful expressions on the mens' faces as they probably recall days long since gone, when fishing was so much simpler.

IN PRAISE OF ESOX LUCIUS

LET'S CLEAR UP a few misconceptions and prejudices about pike. Many anglers look down their collective noses at what they derisively call "alligators," "snakes," and "hammer handles," claiming they are stupid, poor fighters, and lousy tasting. All of which they are not. In Europe, where pike grow much larger than our North American variety, they are considered worthy game fish and excellent table fare.

I also doubt that pike are any less intelligent than other fish. They are, however, more aggressive than most, which probably accounts for their eagerness to grab almost any lure thrown at them— some of which would scare most self-respecting fish out of the water! Although they occa-sionally jump when hooked, don't expect the flashy aerobatics of a rainbow trout or tarpon. Their strike, however, will jolt your arm harder and more vicious-ly than either of these glamour fish. Occasionally you may encounter pike that seem supercharged. They will fight every bit as hard as any muskie, and when finally subdued you will know you have had a battle worth remembering. Pike are solid hitters, good fighters, and excellent table fare. What more could one ask of a fish?

"And what sport doth yield a more pleasing content, and less hurt and change than angling with a hook!"

—Captain John Smith

"I deny altogether that the cold-blooded fish ... is stupid, or slow to learn. On the contrary, fish are remarkably quick, not only under natural conditions, but quick at accommodating themselves to altered circumstances which they could not foresee."

—Richard Jefferies, The Life of the Fields

"Tarpon fishing by night is exciting work, somewhat too exciting for many people."

—J. Turner-Turner

"There is nothing that attracts human nature more powerfully than the sport of tempting the unknown with a fishing line."

—Henry van Dyke

WHAT CONSTITUTES A TROPHY?

AN ANGLER lands a 40-pound chinook salmon from a remote inlet on the West Coast; another catches a 10-inch rainbow trout from a small mountain creek. Which fish is of trophy proportion? While admittedly large, a salmon of that size is less than half the weight chinooks are known to attain (126 pounds). The tiny trout, however, might be a mature adult, and a veritable giant compared to others of its species in that particular creek.

Unlike mammals, fish seldom outgrow their surroundings. Space, not food, is the determining factor. "Dwarf" trout or char found in small creeks—the type we can easily straddle—are often fully grown at five or six inches in length. Given access to more expansive surroundings, they will grow larger. Otherwise, they remain dwarfs.

At twice the size of its neighbors the 10-inch trout would be the true trophy, while that 40-pound salmon might be a mere adolescent that has not yet reached maturity.

However, it's probably safe to say that the "trophy" trout

stands a far better chance of getting released than the "undersized" salmon.

"A TROUT KILLED with a fly is a jewel of price,
But a trout poached with a worm is like
throwing cogged dice."

—J.P. WHEELDON

"THERE IS MUCH to be said, in a world like ours, for taking the world as you find it and for fishing with a worm."

—BLISS PERRY

"YOU WILL FIND angling to be like the virtue of humility, which has a calmness of spirit and a world of other blessings attending upon it."

—IZAAK WALTON, THE COMPLEAT ANGLER

"OF ALL the hardware a fisherman carries with him to the stream, his timepiece is the least important."

—PAUL QUINNETT, DARWIN'S BASS

FISHING
MEMORIES

"OLD FRIENDS can wade a trout
stream together or walk a woodland
cover and not encounter just the
fish or the game of that day, but also
the memories of other days and
other places. They've taken the
bitter with the better and found
it all rewarding."

—LEE WULFF, OUTDOOR LIFE

RAFTING THE GRAND CANYON

THE SON OF a Methodist minister and by all accounts a God-fearing man, John Wesley Powell probably didn't say what I said when he peered over the lip of Badger Creek Rapids to the trough far below. I gulped and bellowed "Holy . . ." in concert with the rest of the passengers. (The last part of the phrase was lost in the roar of the falling water as we dove into the froth.)

The one-armed Powell (he lost an arm at Shiloh) was the first explorer of the Colorado River through the Grand Canyon in 1869. Despite his primitive equipment and inexperience, the only victims of the 1,100-mile ordeal, which began far north on Wyoming's Green River, were three expedition members who climbed out of the canyon and apparently met an Indian war party. They were never seen again.

We hit the trough, and the prow of the 32-foot raft digs in. The river drenches us with icy green water. Powell didn't feel this icy water, and it wasn't green either. There was no Glen Canyon Dam then, gushing frigid water from its base to chill the river below. We are exhilarated by the rapids, feeling we've mutually challenged nature's fury and won. But then I remember that Bobby Kennedy actually *swam* through Badger Creek Rapids.

Canyon fishing is a lightly touched resource. We fish the "bubble line" (the edge of the eddy below rapids where the water curls back on itself) and take trout on spinners. Soon, they will nestle together in a pan, decorated with slices of lime, as we watch the sun dip below the towering face of Red Wall Canyon.

Red Wall Cavern is an enormous bandshell of a shelter cave carved from the sheer wall by eons of silent water. Powell said it would hold 50,000, people and I believe it. Our tiny party is swallowed in its immensity. We stand in awestruck silence. Then, from the back wall, a canyon wren, a bird scarcely bigger than your thumb, begins to sing. The pure, liquid notes swell and fill the natural cup of the cavern, which amplifies it. The wren's song goes on and on; and when it quits, I find that I have been holding my breath for a long time. The Grand Canyon overpowers with its beauty. The canyon wren does the same, though it is only a teardrop in an ocean.

" . . . DON'T WAIT until you retire to go fishing. Don't even wait until your annual vacation. Go at every opportunity. Things that appear more urgent at the moment may, in the long run, turn out to be far less so."

—*TED TRUEBLOOD*, FIELD & STREAM

THE WAY THINGS USED TO BE

ONCE UPON A TIME, you fished with a plug, not a crankbait. "Crankbait" sounds like something you need to change oil (of course, you have to change the plugs, too). And a rowboat used to be a rowboat, not a Metalflake Hawg Chaser Megathrust. It was a rowboat even if you had a motor on it (not an engine, for crying out loud), mainly because the chances were better than 50-50 you'd wind up rowing six miles back to the dock when the motor quit. Docks still are docks, but they didn't float in my day because there was no foam floatation. They were made of unpreserved wood, which meant that at least once a fishing season you plunged through rotting dock decking while carrying a 60-pound outboard motor into ten feet of weed-choked water.

Now, those were the good old days! Newcomers think they invented everything, but, shoot, people had stuff back then just like now—only they didn't survive to tell about it!

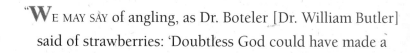

"TWO HONEST and good-natured anglers have never met each other by the way without crying out, 'What luck?'"

—HENRY VAN DYKE, FISHERMAN'S LUCK

"WE MAY SAY of angling, as Dr. Boteler [Dr. William Butler] said of strawberries: 'Doubtless God could have made a better berry, but doubtless God never did'; and so, (if I might be judge), God never did make a more calm, quiet, innocent recreation than angling."

—*Izaak Walton, The Compleat Angler*

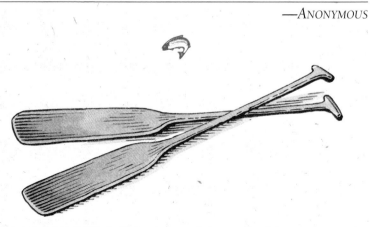

"In this quiet, peaceful time of twilight there is, in this great circle of life, an awful lot of hunting and fishing and catching and killing and dying and eating going on all around me. As the old fisherman said, 'That's the way it is with life. Sometimes you eat well; sometimes you are well-eaten.'"

—*Paul Quinnett, Darwin's Bass*

"Bragging may not bring happiness, but no man having caught a large fish goes home through an alley."

—*Anonymous*

OF FRIENDS AND CANOE TRIPS

I'VE CANOED rivers for more than 30 years. The Ozark streams are my backyard. Their clear waters wash away my sins, whatever they are.

My friend Foster got me into canoeing. We grew up in North Missouri, along muddy streams—little more than drainage ditches, but he'd discovered the sparkling Ozark streams and introduced me to them. So our families canoed and fished together often. We'd set up a communal camp on a broad gravel bar and listen to the whippoorwills and the suck and gurgle of the riffles. Sometimes we caught a few fish, but often just drifted down the river in time suspended. Once Foster and I floated in a blinding snowstorm, fishing the holes for trout and hunting the adjacent fields for quail.

Foster's family and mine made a trip on the Current river one autumn when the leaves were dying and the weather brooded. We floated in sunshine the first day, but mist shrouded the river the next morning and we floated in it all day, past the silent, tall trees and the gray bluffs. It was the last float trip Foster and I made together.

A few years ago, Foster, my friend of nearly 40 years, lost his way to the river. For whatever reason, he couldn't find the peace that we'd always known down on the river, and he took his life. And now all I have are good memories of good trips on good rivers.

"THEY WERE BRIGHT and golden days of sun and sea spray, the salt gritty on your lips, and your nose burning as the sun graved salt into your skin. There were so many things to watch: the way the birds worked the fish, the dorsals of the sharks slicing the water, the dolphins running a match race with the bow of the ship, the porpoises, jocular and friendly, cutting caracoles as they played around the boat, big clownish showoffs happy to have company."

—ROBERT RUARK, THE OLD MAN AND THE BOY

"WE CATCHED FISH and talked, and we took a swim now and then to keep off sleepiness. It was kind of solemn, drifting down the big, still river . . . We had mighty good weather as a general thing, and nothing ever happened to us at all."

—MARK TWAIN, ADVENTURES OF HUCKLEBERRY FINN

"I CHOSE MY CAST, a march-brown and a dun,
And ran down to the river, chasing hope."

—WILFRID S. BLUNT

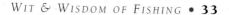

GIVE YOURSELF ENOUGH ROPE . . .

RECENTLY, I jerked on my chain saw starter rope and it came off in my hand. As I looked at the limp and useless thing, I remembered the days when you started an outboard motor that way. With those dinosaurs several things inevitably would happen:

1. The rope would break (along with a couple of your teeth when you socked yourself in the jaw).

2. You pulled to the end of the rope and it didn't retract, dangling like a dead snake.

3. You pulled violently, but the rope had not engaged the thingamajigger, and you dislocated your shoulder.

4. The rope handle slipped out of your fist and somehow flipped up and bloodied your nose.

5. The engine backfired, jerked the rope out of your hand, and you lost an acre of knuckle hide on the engine cowling.

6. The motor caught on fire and somehow, even though the boat was parked in the middle of eight million acre-feet of water, no one could figure out how to extinguish the blaze.

Today's smooth, electronically operated engine is not so much a technological advance as it is a product of survival. So, I looked at the chain saw rope and did the only thing I could do.

I threw it as far as I could.

"(SECOND FISHERMAN) Canst thou catch any fishes then?
(Pericles) I never practised it.
(Second Fisherman) Nay then thou wilt starve, sure;
for here's nothing to be got now-a-days unless
thou canst fish for 't."

—WILLIAM SHAKESPEARE, PERICLES, PRINCE OF TYRE

"OLD NOAH went a-fishing;
He sat upon the ark
And kept his hooks a-dangle
From daybreak on to dark.
His catch was pretty meager;
But every one affirms
He had no chance, because he
Had just a pair of worms."

—ST. CLAIR ADAMS

FROM ONE FLY FISHERMAN TO ANOTHER?

I WAS ON a small stream in Wales, working my way upstream. There was one other angler and I passed him as I flailed fruitlessly at the sleepy water. I tried a combination of every fly I had. I double-hauled and roll-cast and side-armed and did everything else I'd learned over the years. Sometimes I even didn't snag a tree.

That night, in the lodge dining room, my fellow angler of the afternoon approached. He was a classic Scot, spare and frosty of eyebrow, face weathered from a thousand afternoons on the trout stream. If you designed the quintessential trout angler of the bamboo rod era, he would be your model. He gave me a spare smile, the approbation of one old expert to another, and said, "Ye cast a gud line, laddie." I felt ten feet tall.

Except that when I had seen him, he was fishing with worms for eels.

"THEY SAY that the Egyptians are clever in that they rank the eel equal to a god, but in reality it is held in esteem and value far higher than gods, for them we can propitiate with a prayer or two, while to get even a smell of an eel at Athens we may have to spend twelve drachmae or more!"

—ANTIPHANES

"THE CAT-FISH IS a voracious creature, not at all nice in feeding, but one who, like the vulture, contents himself with carrion when nothing better can be had."

—JOHN JAMES AUDUBON

"THE MAN THAT weds for greedy wealth,
He goes a fishing fair,
But often times he gets a frog,
Or very little share."

—UNKNOWN, PEPYSIAN GARLAND

"FOR TROUTS are tickled best in muddy water."

—SAMUEL BUTLER, ON A HYPOCRITICAL NONCONFORMIST

"FOR THE LENGTH of your rod you are always to be governed by the breadth of the river you shall choose to angle at; and for a trout river, one of five or six yards long is commonly enough, and longer it ought not to be, if you intend to fish at ease, and of otherwise, where lies the sport?

CHARLES COTTON

SIMPLE PLEASURES

Brook trout fishing rarely is for trophy-size fish. In most places, a big brook trout has to strain to reach 12 inches, and averages more like eight. But fishing is more than trophies.

I remember my last day on a small stream by a cabin on the edge of the Uncompahgre Wilderness in southwest Colorado. The water was fresh off the snowfields of Sheep Mountain. The stream bounded impatiently from the high mesas, where elk graze and beargrass grows, to a junction with a larger and more thoughtful stream. Three-hundred-foot rock cliffs brooded over the stream valley.

I had returned to the cabin after hiking the high mesa. "One last trout," I murmured, and cast my No. 14 Elk Hair Caddis fly into a swirling eddy pool. The caddis pirouetted twice along the eddy line, and as I lifted the rod a brook trout took it and popped the fly off. I false cast once, seeing the empty line, and sighed, "Well, the trip is over."

As I reeled the empty leader onto the spool, I felt a deep sadness.

"If I was a deacon, I wouldn't let a fish's tail whisk the whole Catechism out of my head."

—HENRY WARD BEECHER

"WHEN THE WIND is in the east,
Then the fishes bite the least;
When the wind is in the west,
Then the fishes bite the best;
When the wind is in the north,
Then the fishes do come forth;
When the wind is in the south,
It blows the bait in the fish's mouth."

—*ANONYMOUS*

"IF I WERE a jolly archbishop,
On Fridays I'd eat all the fish up—
Salmon and flounders and smelts;
On other days everything else."

—*AMBROSE BIERCE*

THE DREAM TRIP

A FRIEND SAVED money for years, shorting his kids, wife, and bird dogs (well, I guess not the bird dogs) so he could travel to Scotland and fish for salmon. His host also was his *gillie* (that is, a fancy scottish word for "guide"). International understanding flowered as they shared single malt Scotch and lied about their fishing prowess. Then they went to the stream and my friend hung a No.2 Jock Scott in his host's ear on the first cast. "Dinna set the hook! Dinna set the hook!" screamed the gillie as he felt the bite . . . but it was too late.

"The rest of the trip went all right," my friend says. "But I noticed that he did his guiding from 90 feet away and off to one side."

"TIS AN employment for my idle time, which is then not idly spent; a rest to my mind, a cheerer of my spirits, a diverter of sadness, a calmer of unquiet thoughts, a moderator of passions, a procurer of contentedness."

—SIR HENRY WOTTON (IZAAK WALTON, THE COMPLEAT ANGLER)

"(Aside) How from the finny subject of the sea
These fishers tell the infirmities of men;
And from their watery empire recollect

All that may men approve or men detect!
(Aloud) Peace be at your labour, honest fisherman."

—WILLIAM SHAKESPEARE, PERICLES, PRINCE OF TYRE

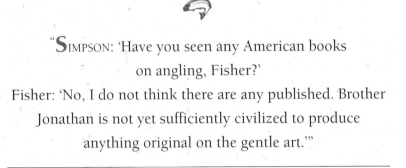

"SIMPSON: 'Have you seen any American books
on angling, Fisher?'
Fisher: 'No, I do not think there are any published. Brother
Jonathan is not yet sufficiently civilized to produce
anything original on the gentle art.'"

—PAUL FISHER

ICE FISHING FOLLY

MY AUNT VIC had the quintessential ice fishing shack in northern Wisconsin. It was her home, and her picture window overlooked a good fishing hole on Big Birch Lake. Anglers would set their tip-ups (a metal flag or other device that pops up or sounds an alarm when a fish takes the bait), come in for a drink and some chit-chat, and watch the tip-ups with one eye and Green Bay football on television with the other.

But more often ice fishing involves an ice fishing shack that looks like an outhouse from Grandma's time—and is just as comfortable, lacking only yellowjackets. Even more primitive is the angler with no protection other than a parka, crouching over an ice fishing hole, back to the wind, shoulders hunched. "Few years back we fished four straight days, 10 hours a day, and the wind chill never got higher than 50 below," one such angler told me.

His face looked like an uncooked flank steak.

"I guess it didn't kill you—you're here," I kidded.

"Oh," he said, "You get used to it."

"THERE WAS A gentle angler who was angling in the sea,
With heart as cool as only heart, untaught of love, can be;
When suddenly the waters rushed, and swelled,
and up there sprung
A humid maid of beauty's mould—
and thus to him she sung:
'Why dost thou strive so artfully to lure my brood away,
And leave them then to die beneath the
sun's all-scorching ray?
Couldst thou but tell how happy are the fish
that swim below,
Thou wouldst with me, and taste of joy which earth can
never know. . . .'
The water rushed, the water swelled,
and touched his naked feet,
And fancy whispered to his heart it was a love-pledge sweet:
She sung another siren lay, more 'wiching than before,
Half-pulled—half plunging—down he sunk, and ne'er was
heard of more."

—JOHANN WOLFGANG VON GOETHE

"THE NICE PEOPLE don't come to the Adirondacks to fish;
they come to talk about the fishing twenty years ago."

—HENRY VAN DYKE

A Blooming Fishing Idiot

SOMETHING ABOUT the first warm day of the year whispers to the spouse, "It's time to clean up," and says to the spouse's spouse, "It's time to go fishing."

I was like a coy spring daffodil, peeping shyly from a snowbank. It was spring, no matter if Willard Scott had warned this daffodil that he would get his buds frosted. Some die-hards catch fish when I'm opening my Christmas presents, but winter fishing is like an addicted reader trapped where the only printed material is the labels on canned goods. No, spring is when you fish, and I would like spring to come a little earlier than it does. Say about December 15.

But my wife has a vastly different approach. "Time to do spring things!" she yodeled joyously. "Like clean out the garage."

I admit, I am afraid of the garage. It is filled with debris too repugnant to leave for the Dispose-All people. (After all, we have an image to maintain.) So we stow the really horrible stuff in the black hole of the garage. I lifted the door and things scuttled into the shadows. Quickly, I plucked a fishing rod and tacklebox from the jumble. "Managed to make a dent in it!" I caroled. "Be back after a while and really get after it!"

I didn't quite hear what she said—something about when pigs fly—but not to worry. It's spring and the fish are rising.

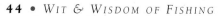

"**A** FRIEND IN TEXAS, to whom I sent a bass-fly and who had never seen a fly before, enthusiastically declared it to be a fish-hook poetized, and thought that a Black bass should take it through a love of the beautiful, if nothing else."

—JAMES HENSHALL

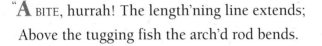

"**A** BITE, hurrah! The length'ning line extends;
Above the tugging fish the arch'd rod bends.

OPPIAN

"**G**IVE ME THE patience to sit calmly by,
While amateurs with veterans gravely vie,
Recounting deeds performed with rod and fly.
Then help me tell the FINAL, CROWNING LIE!"

—C.J. JUDD

"**O**R ALONG THE shallow brooke,
Angling with a baited hooke:
See the fishes leap and play
In a blessed Sunny day."

—NICHOLAS BRETON

WARNING: SHARP OBJECTS

I CONSIDER MYSELF untrustworthy in all manner of knives, and perhaps that's just as well. But, no matter what I do to myself, it's nothing compared to what a friend once did to himself with a filet knife. He was expounding on the problems of the world as he knew them (where to get good bait and the best way to boil crawdads) when a yellowjacket buzzed him. My friend swatted at the insect with his hat . . . and managed to stab the filet knife completely through his biceps. Fortunately, the blade was parallel to all the little muscle fibers, so it slid through, inside to out, with barely a drop of spilled blood.

We insisted that he visit the local doctor. The doctor remarked on the cleanliness of the wound, dressed it, then paused a moment, choosing his words carefully.

"Y'all sure you're gettin' along all right out there?" he asked.

"I WIND ABOUT, and in and out,
With here a blossom sailing,
and here and there a lusty trout,
and here and there a grayling."

—ALFRED TENNYSON

A MAN AT PEACE

I LOOKED AT an old photograph recently. A man faces away from the camera, holding a fly rod. A popping bug dapples the surface of the lake in front of him. The man is so intent, but so completely relaxed that you know here is a person at peace with his world. There is nothing in it but him and the lake and the evening and the ripple of the lure on the still water.

He is my father and I miss him.

"AND IN MINE opinion I could highly commend your orchard, if either through it, or hard by it, there should runne a pleasant River with silver streams; you might sit in your Mount, and angle a speckled Trout or sleighty Eele, or some other dainty fish."

—WILLIAM LAWSON

"LET THE Purist rejoice in the fly that he dries,
And look down on my practice with hauteur,
But for me the surprise
Of the flash of the rise,
The rosy-brown wink under water."

—G.E.M. SKUES

THE ONE THAT GOT AWAY

"I NEVER LOST a little fish—yes,
I am free to say
It always was the biggest fish I caught
that got away."

—*EUGENE FIELD*

THE SEARCH FOR TROPHY TROUT

WHEN TWO- and three-pound cutthroat trout were mentioned, Crony knew he had me hooked. "We'll have to hike a mile and a half, maybe two," he warned, "but it's not bad." I should have known. . . .

The abandoned logging road tunnels through thick stands of alder and second-growth evergreen, climbing at a pitch of 10 or 12 degrees. In less than a quarter mile my breathing progresses from normal to heavy to ragged gasping. Crony cheerfully informs me the grade doesn't vary until we reach the lake.

Sand and gravel have washed off the roadbed, leaving rocks ranging in size from walnuts to bowling balls. Most are round, which makes staying upright a challenge. Which will give out first, my lungs, legs, or flat feet? Crony saunters ahead, patiently waiting during the frequent stops I make to rest and contemplate my sanity.

We finally reach the lake's outlet. The narrow shoreline is littered with dead trees and broken branches, probably the combined results of winds and avalanches. We make our way around, over and under the tangled

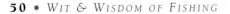

mess, seeking a spot from which to cast. It is slow, treacherous going, but only for 200 yards, where a sheer, impassable cliff looms straight up from the water.

Fish rise sporadically as we rig our ultralight spinning outfits, but the rings are tiny, little more than dimples. Crony catches the first cutthroat and hoists it into the air. It is fully six inches long. He looks puzzled. "I can't figure this out."

"What?"

"How small a three-pounder looks in this light."

We catch a few more, the largest about eight inches long, then call it a day. The opposite shoreline appears much more open and easier to fish, but time has run out.

Later, back at the van, my legs feel like the bones have turned to limp rubber tubing, and my poor flat feet are throbbing, reminding me of what to expect for the next two or three days. As I crawl slowly and painfully behind the wheel, Crony casually asks, "You ever been to Woowoo Lake?"

I shake my head. "Nope."

"Fly fishing only. Big trout—rainbows I hear. Three, four pounds if you hit it right. Supposed to be real good about this time of year. Like to take a look one of these days?"

I turn to stare long and hard at my friend, then croak, "When?"

AN ANGLER'S DOZEN

DURING A MEANDERING, two-week fishing and camping trip in northwestern Quebec, Larry and I stopped in a small village to have lunch and quench our thirst. While seated in the roadside tavern we struck up a conversation with a colorful French-Canadian woodsman. As we enjoyed our ice-cold beer, Edmond regaled us with tales about fishing in the area, pointing out many of the places on a smoke-darkened map that appeared to have been on the wall for many years.

"Here you catch de beeg Dore (walleye)," he said in heavily accented English. He tapped the tip of a work-calloused finger at the appropriate point on a fair-sized lake, then moved it toward a large bay. "And here you get Brochet (pike) as long as your leg."

"How about specks?" asked Larry, using the common Canadian name for brook trout.

"Specks? Truite? Hah! I tell you, you goin' to catch specks till your arms get tired in dis reever here, right where she come into de lake."

"Big ones?" my companion asked.

The wiry little man took a long swallow at his beer, then wiped the moisture from his droopy moustache with the back of his hand. Leaning across the table toward my friend, he said in a quiet, conspiratorial voice, "Beeg, my friend? By golly, de las' time I was dere de fish were so beeg it only take eight of dem to make a dozen!"

"IT MUST, OF COURSE, be admitted that large stories of fishing adventure are sometimes told by fishermen—and why should this not be so? Beyond all question there is no sphere of human activity so full of strange and wonderful incidents as theirs."

—GROVER CLEVELAND

"LYIN' IS lyin', be it about fish or money, and is forbid by Scripter. . . . Billy Matison's got to give up fish-lyin', or he won't never get into the kingdom."

—ELLIS PARKER BUTLER

"WHEN IF AN insect fall (his certain guide)
He gently takes him from the whirling tide;
Examines well his form with curious eyes,
His gaudy vest, his wings, his horns and size,
Then round his hook the chosen fur he winds,
And on the back a speckled feather binds,
So just the colours shine thro' ev'ry part,
That nature seems to live again in art."

—JOHN GAY

WEIGHTY MATTERS

JUST AS organized sports have outstanding professionals and the Olympics its gold, silver, and bronze medalists, recreational anglers have levels of superiority many of us can only dream of reaching. Some are so proficient at "guesstimating" that they can determine the weight of lost fish, even those that are never seen before their escape. Many, it seems, would have established new world records. A few were so large and unyielding in their strength and determination to stay deep, the experts admit that less experienced anglers might have thought they were snagged on the bottom.

"THE TRUTH IS that fishing for trout is as crazy and self-indulgent as inhaling opium. What, then, can be said for trout fishing? Simply this: it's got work beat a mile and is, if a man can stand it, indecently great fun."

—ROBERT TRAVER, ANATOMY OF A FISHERMAN

"HERE COMES the trout that must be caught with tickling."

—WILLIAM SHAKESPEARE, TWELFTH NIGHT

"GOOD SEX AND good fishing both require passion."

—PAUL QUINNETT, DARWIN'S BASS

"THEN COME, my friend, forget your foes,
and leave your fears behind,
And wander forth to try your luck,
with cheerful, quiet mind."

—HENRY VAN DYKE, THE ANGLER'S REVEILLE

"THEY SAY fish should swim thrice . . . first it should swim in the sea (do you mind me?), then it should swim in butter, and at last, sirrah, it should swim in good claret."

—JONATHAN SWIFT, POLITE CONVERSATION

"THAT FISH WILL soon be caught that nibbles at every bait."

—THOMAS FULLER, GNOMOLOGIA

"FOR YOU CATCH your next fish with a piece of the last."

—O.W. HOLMES, VERSES FOR AFTER DINNER

ONE FOR THE RECORD BOOKS

WE HAD BEEN trolling haphazardly around Ontario's Lake Simcoe for two hours when Hotchkiss suddenly barked, "Got one! It's a biggie!"

My friend looked like the proverbial one-armed paper hanger as he held onto his rod with one hand and used his other to reduce the motor's speed and get it out of gear, then crank up the downrigger weight. "I'll tell you," he growled through clenched teeth, "this baby's big—and tough!"

"Muskie?" I asked.

"Don't think so. Gotta be a big laker."

I grabbed a paddle and tried controlling our wind-propelled drift. Hotch eventually started recovering line, but slowly. "It's big," he repeated. "Might even be an IGFA line class record. Got that net ready?"

I picked up the net and peered into the gloom below. Hotch seemed almost in a trance as he pumped and reeled, slowly closing the gap. There it was! I stared, fascinated, as the huge, dark green shape emerged slowly from beneath the boat. I dropped the net and fumbled for my camera. "What are you doing?" screamed Hotch. "Idiot! Get the net!"

I ignored his raving, hoping to capture the expression on his face when Hotch saw he had just spent 15 minutes battling a large, fully opened, plastic garbage bag.

"I SHALL STAY him no longer than to wish . . . that
if he be an honest angler, the east wind may never blow
when he goes a fishing."

—IZAAK WALTON, THE COMPLEAT ANGLER

"IN JULY 1908, a 2,200-pound horned ray was caught
in the Gulf of Mexico. In a moment of classic
understatement, the photo caption informed readers that
this was 'not a pan fish.'"

—FIELD & STREAM

"FOR ANGLING-ROD he took a sturdy oak;
For line, a cable that in storm ne'er broke; . . .
The hook was baited with a dragon's tail—
And then on rock he stood to bob for whale."

—SIR WILLIAM D'AVENANT, BRITANNIA TRIUMPHANS

"IF YOU swear, you will catch no fish."

—ENGLISH PROVERB

ADVENTURES IN BACK-REELING

WHILE CHECKING my buddy Bill's spinning tackle to ensure everything was rigged properly for his first try at steelhead fishing, I tugged on his line, but nothing happened. I pulled harder. Nothing. "Your drag's too tight—like nonexistent."

"I like it tight," he answered.

"What do you do when a fish wants to run?"

"I back-reel 'em."

I stared at him. "Back-reel?"

"Sure. Just reel backwards, but don't give 'em any more line than I have to. I've landed largemouth bass to 14 pounds that way."

"These aren't bucketmouths, Bill, they're steelhead."

"Well, if you don't mind I'll try it my way."

We had fished for nearly two hours when, at the head of the Little Oyster Pool, he got his chance. His bobber floated downstream, its fluorescent red cap cocked slightly forward as the sinker brushed lightly over the bottom. Suddenly, it disappeared.

"Strike!" I barked.

Bill's rod bowed as a mint-bright fish in the mid-teens burst into the air. It splashed down, then streaked straight away, skittering across the surface like a high-powered speedboat. I had never seen anyone back-reel before. It proved interesting. His rod tip snapped downward, then both arms extended as far as he could reach. He tried reeling backwards as he was pulled forward off balance, staggered, then lost his grip on the reel handle. It accelerated instantly, repeatedly striking his fingers and hand with a ratcheting sound similar to a child running a stick along a picket fence. Between that and Bill's high-pitched yelping, it got quite noisy for about four seconds, which was when his line parted with a sharp crack, like a .22 rifle shot.

As Bill waded ashore, his battered hand tucked under his armpit, I asked, "Was that a bit faster than a bucketmouth?"

"You might say that," he admitted. "Faster and stronger."

Bill eventually caught two nice steelhead that day—the first of many over the years—but only after we adjusted the drag on his reel.

"[THE TROUT fisherman] can pause to worship in his own rustic cathedral and listen to an invisible aeolian harp grieving softly amidst its soaring spires."

—ROBERT TRAVER, ANATOMY OF A FISHERMAN

"YOU MUST lose a fly to catch a trout."

—GEORGE HERBERT, JACULA PRUDENTUM

THE SCIENCE OF CLONING

As TIME PASSES, my fishing cronies continue amazing me, especially those who have developed the unbelievable ability to clone their catches. Some only double a single fish or two, but those with more experience are so skilled that they can take a trip totally devoid of anything remotely resembling a bite and convert it into an exciting day filled with fish—all larger than average and all caught and released while fishing alone, out of sight around the river's bend. This is unfortunate, because these fish are always of trophy proportions. (Except, of course, for the occasional, barely legal-sized one they happened to keep because it was badly hooked.)

"Fish or cut bait."

—*Anonymous*

"You cannot bring a hook into a fish's mouth unless there is food on it that pleases him."

—*Juliana Berners*

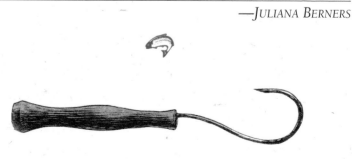

"THE SCIENTIFIC AND GRACEFUL art of throwing the artificial fly is a beautiful accomplishment, but not so difficult as is generally imagined."

—JOHN BROWN

"EVEN A LITTLE KID wouldn't try to catch fish without a sinker. Of course, somebody with no sense might go fishing without a sinker. No rules for fools."

—ANTON CHEKHOV

"THE BEST fish swim near the bottom."

—JOHN CLARKE

"ARTIFICIAL FLIE Angling is the most gentil, ingenious, pleasant and profitable part of the innocent Recreation of Angling; to the perfect Accomplishment of which, is required, not only good affection and frequent practise, but also diligent Observation and considerable Judgement; especially in the choice of Materials and mixing of colours for flies."

—ROBERT HOWLETT

TRUTH OR FICTION?

AFTER A FRIEND returned from a fishing trip in Northern Ontario, he told me this tale. You decide whether or not he told the truth.

"The other guys are hot and heavy into a card game," he said, "so I decide to go out in the canoe. I'm paddling along, trolling a big silver spoon, when all of a sudden I get one heck of a strike. I throw the paddle down and grab for the rod just as it's going over the side, and just in time to see a big pike—20 pounds at least—break water behind the canoe. Now the biggest fish we'd seen so far was only about half that size, so I immediately get visions of winning the pool with that baby—if I get it in.

"Well, that big old momma is really giving me a tussle, when all of a sudden the fight just stops and there's nothing but dead weight on the end of my line. I figure maybe she's fouled in a weed bed or something, so I grab the paddle and start back towards her—hanging onto the rod with one hand and paddling with the other. I'm only about a rod-length away when I spot the fish about four feet down from the surface—crossways in the mouth of the biggest pike I've ever seen! Or heard of! So I did what any red-blooded fisherman would do under the same circumstances—I cut the line and got out of there as fast as I could make that canoe go. Now before you ask why I'd do such a thing, let me explain that there was only about two feet of my fish showing—one foot on each side of that big one's yap.

"You know," he finished off dreamily, reaching for yet another dram of Ye Olde Kidney Convulser, "if they ever put a half-decent road into that place, I might try trailering in a 25-foot boat and take another go at that monster. But in the meantime I ain't going nowhere near that place."

"It is not a fish until it is on the bank."

—*Irish Proverb*

"A visit to a first-class fishing-tackle shop is more interesting than an afternoon at the circus."

—*Theodore Gordon*

"It is self-evident that no fish which inhabit foul or sluggish waters can be 'game fish.' . . .
They may flash with tinsel and tawdry attire; they may strike with the brute force of a blacksmith, or exhibit the dexterity of a prizefighter, but their low breeding and vulgar quality cannot be mistaken."

—*Charles Hallock*

"INCH FOR INCH and pound for pound, [the black bass is] the gamest fish that swims."

—JAMES A. HENSHALL, BOOK OF THE BLACK BASS

"THERE'S NO taking trout with dry breeches."

—CERVANTES, DON QUIXOTE

"EVEN THOUGH competition has no place in fly fishing, and should have none, the angler ought to strive always to play a good game. He should practice the tactics of his art with the same zeal as do the followers of competitive sports if he hopes ever to become an expert fly fisherman in the highest sense of that much misused term."

—GEORGE LA BRANCHE

"NOW FOR THOSE seasons which are nought to angle in, there is none worse than in the violent heat of the day, or when the Winds are loudest, Rain heaviest, Snow and Hail extremest; Thunder and lightning are offensive, or any sharp air which flyeth from the East; the places where men use to wash sheep you shall for bear, for the very smell of the wool will chase fish from their haunts. Land floods are enemies to Anglers, so also at the fall of the leaf is the shedding of leaves into the water, and many other such like pollutions."

—GERVASE MARKHAM

"IT IS NOT easy to tell one how to cast. The art must be acquired by practice."

—CHARLES ORVIS

"THUS USE your frog: put your hook—I mean the arming-wire—through his mouth and out at his gills, and then with a fine needle and silk sew the upper part of his leg with only one stitch to the arming-wire of your hook, or tie the frog's leg above the upper joint to the armed wire; and in so doing, use him as though you loved him"

—IZAAK WALTON, THE COMPLEAT ANGLER

FISHING LESSONS

"ANGLING MAY be said to be so like the mathematics that it can never be fully learnt."

—IZAAK WALTON,
THE COMPLEAT ANGLER

STARTING OUT

FISHING IS AN evolutionary process. Kids often start out dunking worms for trout in small creeks, crickets for panfish, or pieces of clam for shiners off seaside wharfs. Some folks are older—even adults—before they take up fishing, perhaps cane-poling for panfish, trolling for salmon or lake trout, or casting lures for pike or largemouth bass. The point is, few anglers start out as fly-fishers, but somewhere along the way almost all will entertain thoughts of challenging their prey with a fly rod.

Unfortunately, most never get past the thinking stage, avoiding fly-fishing in the belief it is simply too difficult and mysterious to tackle. In all likelihood they have listened to, or read something written by various "experts"—often self-appointed—who have conveniently blotted out their own first, pathetic attempts at fly-casting. The sort who indulge in pompous pontificating about the "science and art" necessary to match wits with finned creatures that are seemingly empowered with great levels of intelligence.

The truth is: Fish possess tiny brains that preclude anything approaching mental acuity. They react more by reflex than any other trait, but they do develop caution in heavily fished waters, and can be maddeningly selective feeders when food is abundant. However, I have yet to hear of any trout swimming around with magnifying glasses so they can count the number of hackle fibres in a nymph's tail, or using rulers to measure the length of leader tippets.

Forget the egotists. There is nothing mystical or magical about fly-fishing . . . nothing. It is simply one of many facets that make up recreational fishing. Being a fly-fisher won't make you "better than" or "superior to" other anglers, but it will provide you with an interesting, challenging, and satisfying way to pursue most fish species.

If you never progress beyond the duffer stage, so what? Fishing is supposed to be fun. Enjoy it. If you happen to become proficient, fine, but do me a favor: enjoy your new-found expertise and strive to become even better.

But never, ever forget your roots.

"CARP suck. They slurp down food with a sound suggestive of a drunk walking his lips through beer puddled on a Formica bar. It is an obnoxious, vaguely obscene noise, fully befitting a carp, which to many is an obnoxious, vaguely obscene fish. Trout rise and sip. Bass leap and inhale. Carp just suck."

—LIONEL ATWILL, SPORTS AFIELD

"THERE AIN'T but one time to go fishin' and that's whenever you can."

—DIRON TALBERT

Do Scents Make Sense?

THE PRACTICE of using scents to attract fish is lost in history, but might well have originated through the use of "chumming"—throwing ground-up bait into the water. Then again, it might have been the first time a fisherman spit on his bait. Whatever the origins, various concoctions have been around for years, most common of which is oil of anise.

The modern line of scents we use today appeared during the late 1970s, then started attracting serious attention in the early 1980s. There have been some notable advances, but also some better-forgotten duds. About 1978, while living in Ontario, I was given a slim, minnow-shaped plug to field test. It bore a slight resemblance to an original Rapala, but its porous plastic body was said to be impregnated with some magic elixir the enclosed advertising brochure claimed would "REVOLUTIONIZE FISHING!!" (Their words, not mine.)

I cast and trolled that plug in stretches of the Rideau River known to be virtually crawling with fish, and finally caught a stunted little rock bass. It was hooked in the anus. This was duly reported to the manufacturer, along with a suggestion that the fish might have been making a social comment about the worth of their lure.

For some reason they never sent me anything else to field test.

"For eels and wild ducks, put hooks upon warp or line, about a foot apart, and the same length to each hook; put a gudgeon on one hook, and a piece of lights on the other all the way. The lights will swim, which the ducks will take, and the eels will take the gudgeons; so, when you draw the line out, you will have a duck on one hook and an eel on the other. This you will find to be excellent sport."

—John Mayer

"If you carry pipe cleaners in your fishing jacket you will never be without a trout lure, even if you lose your fly box. A cleaner twisted around the shank of a hook looks much like a nymph. You can enhance the illusion by coloring it with coffee, a ballpoint pen, or the juices of mashed bugs and flies."

—H.G. Tapply, Field & Stream

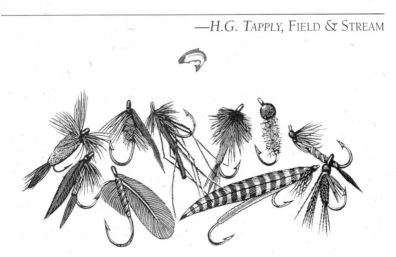

What an Angler Really Means Is . . .

THERE'S REALLY an art to the interpretation of the way anglers speak. For instance, if an angler tells his wife, "I'm off to Gruntle's Tackle Emporium to pick up a few things," what he really means is: "I'm buying a new tackle box the size of a Dodge cube van, then filling it with necessities." And when speaking to another angler, the phrase "You shouldn't need waders" really means, "That river dries up this time of year."

When doing your own transla-
tions, it is important to remember: never jump to conclusions. If you are planning a summertime trip to the Quintessential River and you are advised, "When I spent a week on the Quint' last year,

we didn't have to use our sunscreen once," you might assume this really means, "It rained every day." You would be wrong. What it actually means is, "The clouds of mosquitoes were so thick that the sunlight couldn't penetrate them." You must be vigilant about watching for these variances of meaning in order to avoid confusion. Experience will teach you that had there actually been torrential rains throughout his entire trip, he would have said, "You might find the river's a tad high that time of year, but there won't be any mosquitoes."

"AND FOR the principal point of angling,
always keep yourself away from the water and from
the sight of the fish—far back on the land or else behind
a bush or a tree—so that the fish may not see you.
For if he does, he will not bite."

—JULIANA BERNERS

"AND ETE THE olde fishe, and leve the young,
Though they moore towghe be uppon the tonge."

—PIERS OF FULHAM

"... TO FISH fine and far off is the first and principal rule
for trout angling."

—CHARLES COTTON

"SINCE BASS were feeding in the lily pads during
the time of the dinosaurs and no doubt gobbled up some
of my direct ancestors, I'll sharpen this hook a bit, and
remind any bass listening, a la Schwarzenegger,
'What goes around comes around, baby.'"

—PAUL QUINNETT, DARWIN'S BASS

THE PECKING ORDER

RECREATIONAL anglers fit into one of two groups: casual and dedicated. But there is a variable, often imperceptible transition level between them. The first group treats fishing as restful relaxation to help unwind from the daily grind, get some fresh air, and maybe catch a fresh fish now and then for the table. The latter group takes it much more seriously, and some—quite a few, really—become involved to the point of fanatic obsession. When not fishing as often as possible, they read about it; talk about it; watch videos; attend courses, symposiums, and clinics; and join clubs with members who have similar interests.

The problem is, no matter which group we belong to, we cause confusion by creating categories that are further complicated with self-imposed rules and restrictions. The use of open-faced spinning reels classifies anglers as amateurs to people wielding level-wind models, while they in turn are scorned by those who have mastered casting with single-action reels. Collectively, all are held in haughty disdain as bait-dunking, hardware-chucking buffoons by the fly-fishing fraternity, a streak of prejudice that continues even within their own ranks. Dry fly purists look down their noses at those who fling wet flies; chironomid anglers accuse anyone who uses leech patterns as being little better than worm fishermen; rainbow trout worshippers won't lower themselves to fly-fish for bass; and steelheaders classify all other salmonids as coarse fish.

True, most of this is simply good-natured, verbal jousting between friends who fish together, but some misguided souls actually take it seriously. Conceited people like these are best avoided as they are seldom any fun to fish with. Besides, their arrogance might well be contagious, and we already have too many snobs within our ranks.

"You see the way the Fisherman doth take
To catch the fish; what Engins doth he make?
Behold how he ingageth all his wits,
Also his Snares, Lines, Angles, Hooks and Nets."

—John Bunyan, The Pilgrim's Progress

"It was thought she was a woman and was turned into a cold fish."

—William Shakespeare, Winter's Tale

"But what is the test of a river? 'The power to drown a man,' replies the river darkly."

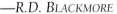

—R.D. Blackmore

BACK TO BASICS

IF YOU are hesitant about learning to fly-cast, don't be. Some folks learn quickly; others must work harder at it. I taught myself nearly 50 years ago, using an *Outdoor Life* propped open on a nearby stump so I could see the illustrations showing the various rod positions.

The basics came blessedly easy for a clumsy 14-year-old with motor skills that appeared to verge on terminally maladroit. By midsummer, I considered myself quite the hotshot, but reality set in while watching two young boys fly-fishing from a nearby resort dock. Their tackle was far superior to mine, and their casting was so stylish I felt like slinking away and hiding. But I stayed, watched, introduced myself, and picked up some useful pointers.

It probably looked strange to see a gangly teenager taking lessons from a seven- and nine-year-old, but it was a fair exchange. I showed them how to catch redside shiners with tiny pieces of worm on a single egg hook. All they had ever done was fly-fish for trout, so they found it was great fun.

"FISH AND guests in three days are stale."

—JOHN LYLY, EUPHUES

"UNLESS YOU married someone who is as crazy about fishing as you are, then you already know how sex and fishing can come to conflict and grief."

—PAUL QUINNETT, DARWIN'S BASS

"UNLESS A MAN makes a fly to counterfeit that very fly in that place, he is like to lose his labour. . . .
Three or four flies neat and rightly made and not too big, serve for a Trout in most rivers, all the summer."

—IZAAK WALTON, THE COMPLEAT ANGLER

"CRICKETS MAKE EXCELLENT bait for bass and panfish, and bread and sugar make excellent bait for crickets. Sprinkle the bread with sugar, moisten slightly, and leave on the ground overnight beneath cloth or newspaper.
You should collect a day's supply of bait."

—H.G. TAPPLY, FIELD & STREAM

"WHAT A SHAME and pity is then, that such a river should be destroyed by the basest sort of people."

—CHARLES COTTON

READ ALL ABOUT IT

A BOOK STORE manager recently confided that the only non-fiction topics outselling fly-fishing titles were cookbooks and sex manuals! Thousands of books have been written about fly-fishing, and some are classics. Most private collections contain at least some works by Roderick Haig-Brown, Charles Ritz, Lee Wulff, Arnold Gingrich, A.J. McClane, Ray Bergman, Robert Traver, Joe Brooks, and Norman Maclean—all, alas, now departed. There are, however, plenty of excellent writers still alive and turning out entertaining and informative works, among them Nick Lyons, John Gierach, A.D. Livingston, Jack Shaw, Charles Waterman, Steve Raymond, Brian Chan, and Lefty Kreh.

While a book might be anecdotal rather than instructional, you will generally learn something of value. No matter how skilled and experienced one becomes, the learning process is never-ending. I have friends now in their 80s and 90s who are held in high esteem as expert fly-fishers and tiers, yet their level of interest in learning new techniques remains undiminished, as does their curiosity about how others accomplish things, whether casting on the water or creating at the fly-tying vise. One can never outgrow what a joy it is to learn—or to teach others your own secret fishing tricks.

"WHEN WE HAVE good luck we come home early; otherwise we stay late and fight it out. How often we are defeated! Everything goes against us and we struggle in vain to conquer adverse conditions, but if we do win out, how pleased we are. We really believe that we can fish."

—*THEODORE GORDON*

"THE MUSE has always smiled on anglers . . . while seeking the sources of their bright streams, they find, in some magical way, the holy and secret sources of poetry also, so that when they tell of rivers and water meadows they speak with the tongues of angels; or perhaps there is some similarity about making a cast and making a sentence— both must be accurate, graceful, rhythmical and neat."

—*JOHN MOORE*

"MOSQUITOES CAN take the fun out of still-fishing from an anchored boat when there is no breeze to keep them away. Next time, take along a box of moth-repellent flakes and scatter them over the bottom of the boat. It tends to discourage them."

—*H.G. TAPPLY, FIELD & STREAM*

A TIME FOR FISHING

SPRING IS MY favorite time to fish for steelhead. The silvery sea-run rainbow trout are seldom plentiful, for low water often keeps all but a few impatient ones milling about the river mouths. Those trouts daring enough to venture into the shallow streams are wary and nervous, difficult to catch. However, during this period of transition, winter-darkened forests slowly come alive with sights, sounds, and scents as days grow longer and leaden skies yield to canopies of cobalt blue.

The salmonberry bushes are first to bud in our area, and soon a profusion of their pale pink blossoms brighten the river banks. Next are the bright-yellow skunk cabbage, rising like hooded cobras from the swampy forest floor. Then, as if by magic, the mossy carpet beneath the towering trees is patterned with delicate white trilliums, each as fragile and beautiful as any orchid.

Birds also favor spring, and from every tree they seem to compete in a contest to determine which can sing the sweetest song. Robins, thrushes, finches, siskins, warblers, wrens, and chickadees—just to name a few—all joyously announcing winter has finally ended for another year. Yes, the fishing is definitely slower during the spring than in winter, but somehow it doesn't really matter.

"Swivels have a habit of hiding in the corners of your tackle box, and it's hard to dig them out when you want one. Instead of carrying them loose, string them on either a paper clip or safety pin. Then when you need one you can find it fast."

—*H.G. Tapply*, Field & Stream

"If he prove a large fish, pull not, but hold your rod still, the butt end outward towards the fish, til you can turn him as one would turn an unruly horse. But if he will run out a stretch, and you cannot follow him, then if the place be clear, throw your rod in after him, and commend all to Fortune, rather than lose hook, line, and fish."

—*Robert Howlett*

WHO'S INACTIVE AND BORING?

"FRANKLY, I don't understand what people see in fishing," the tanned, dapper-looking man said to me at a cocktail party. "Boring, and much too inactive for me."

My mind flashed back to midday, when I trudged around the bend of the small stream to see Crony standing on the rotting trunk of a fallen red cedar tree. He held his index finger to his lips, then pointed to the water below. I moved closer, staying well back from the water's edge, then climb stealthily up the fallen tree's ramplike trunk.

The stream was low and crystal clear. With the sun blazing almost directly overhead I could see each rock and pebble below. A tapestry of pastel colours illuminated by water and sunlight: various shades of rose, maroon, green, blue, gray, light tan, dark brown, with here and there the stark white of pieces of quartz and the jet black of coal from a seam upstream.

I spotted the male steelhead immediately. Big! At least 15 pounds. The sides of his deep body were silver, but a faint blush of pink was beginning to show along the lateral line and gill covers. His back was brown, flecked with black and gold. A truly handsome creature—for the time being. Within a few short days the bright chrome mantle would change to flaming scarlet as he reverted to his rainbow trout coloration; the hook in his jaw would become pronounced; his well-muscled body would become gaunt and scarred and ragged of fin from the spawning ritual. But for the present he was a real trophy.

"Where's the hen?"

"Directly upstream about 30 feet."

I finally saw her snugged up against a large boulder. "Wow! That is a big fish."

"Yeah. I figure 18, maybe 20 pounds."

"You going to try for them?"

"No." He slowly shook his head. "I haven't the heart to break up such a loving couple. Besides, just think of the beautiful babies they'll make if they manage to get on the spawning beds."

Envisioning a school of 20-pound fish swarming into this small river made me smile.

I was still smiling as I snapped out of my reverie. I glanced at the golf club crest on the fellow's blazer, then replied, "Yes, well, different strokes and all that I suppose." Then I excused myself and wandered off in search of a kindred soul.

"MEN CALL Salmon 'capricious'; but is not the term a cover for their own ignorance about the habits of the fish and the flies they show them, rather than the truthful representation of facts?"

—GEORGE KELSON

"**Y**ET RESPECTABLE-LOOKING, even wise-looking people were fixing bits of worms on bent pieces of wire to catch trout. Sport they called it. Should church-goers try to pass the time fishing in baptismal fonts while dull sermons were being preached, the so-called sport might not be so bad; but to play in the Yosemite temple, seeking pleasure in the pain of fishes struggling for their lives, while God himself is preaching his sublimest water and stone sermons!"

—JOHN MUIR

"**N**EXT TIME you hook a fly in your shirt or jacket, try this method of working it free without tearing the fabric: stick a pin through the cloth where the hook entered and use it as a wedge to force the fabric away from the barb. Then carefully back the hook out."

—H.G. TAPPLY, FIELD & STREAM

"No HIGH AMBITION may I claim—
I angle not for lordly game
Of trout, or bass, a wary bream—
A black perch reaches the extreme
Of my desires; and goggle-eyes
Are not a thing that I despise;
A sunfish, or a chub or cat—
A silver-side—yea, even that!"

—JAMES WHITCOMB RILEY

"ONE OF THE best things about trout fishing is going back to a familiar place. Then the woods welcome a man. It is not like being alone on a strange river."

—GORDON MACQUARRIE

"YOUR BAIT of falsehood takes this carp of truth."

—WILLIAM SHAKESPEARE, HAMLET

"IF YOU were to make little fishes talk,
they would talk like whales."

—JAMES BOSWELL

TRUE STORIES

"SOMEBODY JUST BACK of you while you are fishing is as bad as someone looking over your shoulder while you write a letter to your girl."

—ERNEST HEMINGWAY

How Big Was It?

FISHING LORE IS liberally spiced with tales of gigantic fish possessing monumental eating habits. Some are out-and-out myths, but others—hard as they are to believe—often turn out to be factual. One of the most famous fish stories dates back to 1497, when the skeleton of a huge pike was displayed at Mannheim Cathedral, in the German province of Wurttemburg. Known as the "Emperor's Pike," the impressive trophy measured 19 feet long, and was said to have weighed 550 pounds when caught. It was not until the 19th century that a skeptic pointed out most of the gigantic fish's length was constructed from the mid-sections of several different pike. Alas, The Emperor's Pike has since been known as "The Mannheim Hoax."

With a fish story like that to live up to, it is of little wonder that European folklore abounds with tales of monstrous pike—all much larger than the Emperor's Pike, of course. Some are said to have dragged screaming swimmers to their watery graves, others gobbled down full-grown swans as appetizers, and a few even grabbed mules, horses, and other livestock by their respective snouts while they drank, then tried dragging them into the water. Almost all of these leviathans were supposedly hooked by anglers, but none were ever landed. It appears that even back then, the big ones always got away.

Every few years, tales of man-eating fish in Iliamna Lake on the Alaska Peninsula are resurrected, stories of hapless travelers having their kayaks and canoes swamped, then ending up as snacks for the giant fish said to dwell in the lake's mysterious depths. Handed down through generations of native people, this legend continues, with disappearances on the big lake still attributed to the gigantic denizens which supposedly dwell there. Adding fuel to these stories are occasional reports by aircraft pilots of sighting huge "marine creatures" cruising Iliamna's waters. Hmm . . . anyone for swimming in Iliamna Lake?

"THE MOTION PICTURE masterpiece of all times awaits the actor who can even partially duplicate the flaming dramatic power and indomitable fighting spirit of sportdom's most magnificent adversary. Truly, Germany's dream of a race of supermen would be realized if the driving power of humans could be fashioned as is that of the swordfish."

—CECIL B. DeMILLE, FIELD & STREAM

"ANGLING IS SOMEWHAT like poetry, men are to be born so . . . It is an art worthy the knowledge and patience of a wise man."

—IZAAK WALTON, THE COMPLEAT ANGLER

THE STATE OF FISHING

MOST STATES have official state flowers or trees, but only 29 have an official state fish. Bass and trout predominate. Wisconsin's fish is the muskellunge, Minnesota's the walleye. Massachusetts, long dependent on the fishing industry, celebrates the cod and a carving of a codfish has hung in the State House since 1784, giving it the distinction of being the oldest designated state fish in the nation.

Some states have discussed a state fish, but not been able to pick one. Kansas proposed both the channel catfish, a common species, and the Topeka shiner (named for the state capital), an endangered species. But nothing happened. Missouri periodically eyes potential state fish, but the vociferous advocates of largemouth bass, smallmouth bass, rainbow trout, and bluegill always shoot down each other's candidates, one by one. In some cases, the state fish seems to have been overlooked. Louisiana has a state tree, insect, flower, and even a dog—but no state fish.

Most state fish have been designated by the legislature, but not all. Illinois took a democratic approach and let schoolchildren choose. They picked the valiant bluegill. However, many of the votes were for the class clown, the school principal, or some teacher the kids didn't like. Hawaii also chose a state fish by ballot. Apparently there was much ballot box stuffing. The winner was the "humuhumunukunukuapua'a" (a pig-nosed trigger fish), mostly because of the length of its name. Embarrassed officials let the designation expire after five years and there haven't been any popular votes since.

"THE GREAT CHARM of fly-fishing is that we are always learning; no matter how long we have been at it, we are constantly making some fresh discovery, picking up some new wrinkle. If we become conceited through great success, some day the trout will take us down a peg."

—THEODORE GORDON

"BUT PERHAPS the unkindest polluters of all are those fellow fishermen who themselves add to the growing mounds of beer cans and broken glass that increasingly adorn our lakes and streams. It is probably true that few fish were ever slain by flying beer cans, but their gleaming presence in trout waters surely kills enjoyment, the precious illusion of space and pastoral solitude and simple pine-laden cleanliness, and above all the wavering illusion that men were not entirely descended from the wild hog."

—ROBERT TRAVER, ANATOMY OF A FISHERMAN

A LURKING LUNKER

A MODERN, TWO-STORY house rests on a large raft at an Atlantic salmon farm near Port Hardy, British Columbia. The bottom floor contains a laboratory and storage area, while the top floor has comfortable living quarters. With time to kill while his supper cooked, one of the workers was fishing off the second story balcony. When the stove's timer went off, he left his jig in the water, walked into the living room, then tied his line around the wooden arm of a settee. A minute or two later, he heard a scraping noise in the living room. He turned around to see the settee skitter across the floor and crash into the sliding door, breaking the glass. It then went through the doorway and hit the balcony railing, smashing part way through it before the line broke. He later told charter boat captain Ian Andersen that he just stood there with his mouth hanging open, wondering what kind of fish was big enough to do that kind of damage.

The mystery was solved three weeks later, when one of Andersen's customers landed a 200-pound pacific halibut right beside the fish farm. It still had the fish farm worker's Norwegian jig stitched to its jaw!

"I'VE BEEN attracted by deep-sea fishing for many years, but somehow I never got around to it. It seems like every time I planned to go, something annoying would come up to prevent it, like root canal or a job. But early in November of

1968—it was shortly before Election Day—I looked over the list of presidential candidates and it was clear to me that if ever there was a time for a man to go fishing, this was it."

—MAX SHULMAN, FIELD & STREAM

"I HAD A STRONG TASTE for angling, and would sit for any number of hours on the bank of a river or pond watching the float."

—CHARLES DARWIN

"WE ARE WAITING for the long-promised invasion. So are the fishes."

—WINSTON CHURCHILL, RADIO BROADCAST TO THE FRENCH PEOPLE, OCTOBER 21, 1940

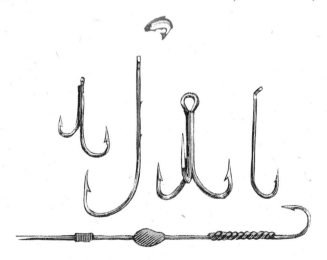

THE FISHING PRESIDENTS

MOST PRESIDENTS dabble in fishing if they fish at all. It has been said that Harry Truman was most likely to fish if there was a camera present and it was an election year. Calvin Coolidge said fishing was for old men and boys, ticking off fishing voters. Then he learned to fish . . . with worms. Fly anglers were enraged. But he finally got a fly rod and learned to use it—too well. He once bragged to game wardens in Wisconsin that he had caught 26 trout. But the limit was 25. Everyone grew silent and looked at their shoetops. Mr. Coolidge acted presidential: "You boys decide," he said. Not surprisingly there was no ticket issued.

Herbert Hoover, an accomplished fly fisherman, ribbed his fellow Republican: "President Coolidge apparently had not fished before election," Mr. Hoover wrote. "Being a fundamentalist in religion, economics, and fishing, he began his fish career for common trout with worms. Ten million fly fishermen at once evidenced disturbed minds. Then Mr. Coolidge took to a fly. He gave the Secret Service guards great excitement in dodging his backcast and rescuing flies from trees."

Grover Cleveland was a fierce devotee of the smallmouth bass. Mr. Cleveland wore out those who fished with him. A friend, Richard Gilder, commented, "he will fish through hunger and heat, lightning and tempest." Two friends, Gilder and actor Joe Jefferson, once watched Mr. Cleveland fish one hot midday on Cape Cod. As They lolled on the bank, watching Mr. Cleveland flail the water, undeterred by heat or slack fishing, Jefferson turned to Gilder and said, "Well, it is lucky for us that you and I can do something besides fish!"

"'THE THING ABOUT fishing,' the Old Man said,
'is not how many fish you catch or what kind of fish.
I, for one, think that making a hardheaded profession
out of fishing is a waste of time, because a fish is only a fish,
and when you make a lot of work out of him you lose the
whole point of him.'"

—*ROBERT RUARK*, THE OLD MAN AND THE BOY

"YE MONSTERS of the bubbling deep,
Your Maker's praises spout;
Up from the sands ye codlings peep,
And wag your tails about."

—*COTTON MATHER*, HYMN

"SEE HOW HE throws his baited lines about,
And plays his men as anglers play their trout."

—*O.W. HOLMES*, THE BANKER'S SECRET

HE HAD IT ALL WRONG

NO MATTER WHERE or how anglers choose to fish, there are usually well-known flies, lures, or baits to use and specific tactics that are proven to work better than others. However, nothing is ever carved in stone. General Sir Charles Loewen, former Adjutant General of the British Army, once told me about fishing for Atlantic salmon in Northern Ireland during the early 1930s.

"I decided to fish a river that bordered the garrison I was commanding," he said. "When I arrived at the river, my 'batman' (an officer's servant) was there, fishing a deep pool. I noticed a cork bobber on the water, so I asked him what he was fishing for. He said he was fishing for salmon. I asked what he was using on his line, and he said a worm. Well, it was obvious the poor fellow knew nothing about fishing for salmon, 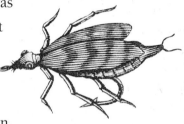 so I went into a lengthy discourse about how salmon didn't feed when they returned to the rivers, and could only be taken with lures or flies. He reeled in while I was talking, and when I finally finished rambling on he thanked me for my information, then bid me good afternoon. He then walked over to a nearby tree, picked up two absolutely beautiful salmon of about 15 and 20 pounds, and walked off without another word."

"Give me mine angle; we'll to the river: there,
My music playing far off, I will betray
Tawny-finn'd fishes; my bended hook shall pierce
Their slimy jaws."

—William Shakespeare, Antony and Cleopatra

"Simon Peter saith unto them, I go a fishing.
They say unto him, We also go with thee."

—New Testament: John 21:3

"Immense, of fishy form and mind,
Squamous, omnipotent, and kind;
And under that Almighty Fin,
The littlest fish may enter in.
Oh! never fly conceals a hook,
Fish say, in the eternal Brook,
But more than mundane weeds are there,
And mud, celestially fair."

—Rupert Brooke, Heaven

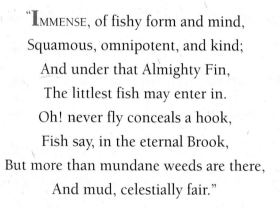

ART OR SCIENCE?

OUR LATE EVENING DISCUSSION concerning the "art and science" of fly-fishing was well-laced with technical jargon. Through it all, the oldest and most respected member of our group sat quietly until someone thought to ask his views.

"Well," Jack replied, "I figure it's all based on percentages: One percent water conditions, one percent light conditions, one percent having the right pattern, one percent proper positioning, one percent presentation, and 95 percent whether the fish feel like biting."

"THE END OF FISHING is not angling, but catching."

—THOMAS FULLER, GNOMOLOGIA

"ANGLERS HAVE been known to use weird baits throughout time, but in 1911, two anglers came up with the ultimate home-grown concoction—their noses. In May 1911, we reported on an ice fisherman who put his face low to the hole long enough for a 14-inch pickerel to jump out of the water and grab the tip of his 'beezer.'

In the following issue, a letter appeared from an angler who had become thirsty, put his face to the water for a drink, and felt a twinge. When he pulled his face away from the water he noticed that his nose appeared to have grown a foot—an 11-inch rainbow had mistaken his sunburned nose for a scarlet ibis.

The trout fisherman assured all that his nose was healing nicely, and he had since bought a drinking cup."

—FIELD & STREAM

"EXCEPT TO HEFT my father's fly rod as a kid in Michigan, I'd never even held such a rod in my hand, much less waded a stream. And while I thought I'd done a lot of fishing, I didn't even know that real angling begins where mere fishing leaves off, the moment you step into a stream with a fly rod in your hand."

—ARNOLD GINGRICH, FIELD & STREAM

"IT IS HARD to wait for the strike when the light is failing and the tick of the ten-second countdown passes slowly. And yet, there is this delicious tension—this tension that fills the body with hope and anticipation. It is an ancient excitement, and it answers one of the whys of angling. The tension in a fishing line runs both ways."

—PAUL QUINNETT, DARWIN'S BASS

THIS RECORD COULD STAND FOREVER

MANY ANGLERS consider the Tyee Club of British Columbia the world's most exclusive fishing club. Located at Campbell River, B.C., neither fortune nor fame will gain you membership; it must be earned. According to Tyee Club regulations, in order to qualify for membership, an angler must land a chinook salmon weighing 30 pounds or more while fishing from a rowed boat. The rod must be between six and nine feet in length, and line must test no stronger than 20 pounds. The fish must be caught on an artificial lure that can have only one single hook attached, and until such time that the fish is netted, absolutely no assistance can be given to the angler.

In early August, 1987, then six-year-old Brian Kruse of Campbell River became the club's youngest member by hooking and landing a 39-pound chinook salmon. A 78-pound youth catching a fish weighing half of his own body weight is impressive; that he did so unassisted would be hard to believe had the entire 45-minute battle not been witnessed by several anglers in nearby boats. Although Brian's father was rowing the boat, he did not lend a hand until it was time to net the fish. While records are made to be broken, the one set by Brian Kruse borders on impossible.

"NICK LOOKED DOWN into the pool from the bridge. It was a hot day. A kingfisher flew up the stream. It was a long time since Nick had looked into a stream and seen trout. They were very satisfactory. As the shadow of the kingfisher moved up the stream, a big trout shot upstream in a long angle, only his shadow marking the angle, then lost his shadow as he came through the surface of the water, caught the sun, and then, as he went back into the stream under the surface, his shadow seemed to float down the stream with the current, unresisting, to his post under the bridge where he tightened facing up into the current.
Nick's heart tightened as the trout moved.
He felt all the old feeling.
He turned and looked down the stream. It stretched away, pebbly-bottomed with shallows and big boulders and a deep pool as it curved away around the foot of a bluff."

—*ERNEST HEMINGWAY*, BIG TWO-HEARTED RIVER

RANK HAS ITS PRIVILEGE

FORMER PRESIDENT George Bush, an ardent angler, once was mightily embarrassed when everyone in his party caught fish on his vacation and he didn't. Newspapers kept a box score: "Fish 14, Bush 0." But Presidents always have the last word.

Once, Mr. Bush was aboard a party boat on a Montana lake with several rods out, trolling for lake trout. Suddenly, one outrigger tripped and the rod began to buck up and down. "Fish on!" someone shouted.

"Is that my rod?" exclaimed Mr. Bush excitedly.

An aide, mindful that Mr. Bush was the ranking figure on board, said with consummate tact, "Mr. President, they're ALL your rod!"

"THE WOODS are made for the hunters of dreams,
The brooks for the fishers of song."

—SAM FOSS

"THE CLIMAX in the poem of trouting is the spring of the split bamboo."

—LEWIS FRANCE

"Once an angler, always a fisherman. If we cannot have the best, we will take the least, and fish for minnows if nothing better is to be had."

—*Theodore Gordon*

"You must not be too greedy in catching your said game [fish], as in taking too much at one time. . . . That could easily be the occasion of destroying your own sport and other men's also."

—*Juliana Berners*

"All that are lovers of virtue, and dare trust in His providence, and be quiet, and go a-angling."

—*Izaak Walton, The Compleat Angler*

"I am fond of all sorts of fishing, in fresh or salt water, in the interior of the country, or on the coast, but trout angling takes a grip on the imagination. It is more of a mental recreation than other methods."

—*Theodore Gordon*

TWO VIEWS OF FISHING

I AM STANDING BY THE window of our rental cottage, savoring the day's first cup of coffee, when two young men cruise by in a sleek bass boat. The driver studies a chart, glancing up occasionally to take bearings, while his partner assembles several rods and stows them in gunwale-mounted holders. As they cruise slowly from sight around a nearby island, the driver is still hunched over his chart, while the other fellow is now fiddling with the instrument-laden console. I smile. Fishing is serious business.

I'm on my second cup of coffee when two old fellows appear on the dock. One is tall and slender, with a thatch of white hair jutting from beneath a misshapen straw hat, the other is shorter, and as rotund as his friend is lean. They appear to be in their late sixties, probably older.

The tall man carries two spinning outfits, a small tackle box, and a large canvas rucksack, the other totes an identical tackle box and a metal minnow bucket. They stop by a neatly painted, flat-bottom rowboat, climb in with slow, stiff caution, then load their gear. When last seen, they are rounding the same island, the chubby fellow pulling easily on the oars, his companion lounging on the rear seat, puffing contentedly on his pipe and sipping from the red top of his vacuum jug.

I chuckle as I turn from the window. The anglers in the bass boat will probably take more fish—but those in the rowboat will probably have more fun.

ZANE GREY—ANGLER?

MOST KNOW Zane Grey as a famous western writer. More than 130 million copies of his books have been sold. As late as 1977, 38 years after his death, a "new" book appeared from discovered material. But most don't know that Grey was the best-known fisherman of his time, the 1920s and 1930s. He held countless world saltwater records and even made a movie, "White Death," about the great white shark long before "Jaws" came along. Grey died of a massive heart attack in October, 1939—probably brought on by having had an exhausting battle with an 800-pound great white shark the previous February.

"AND THE MIGHTY sturgeon, Nahma,
Said to Ugudwash, the sun-fish,
To the bream, with scales of crimson,
'Take the bait of this great boaster,
Break the line of Hiawatha!'"

—HENRY WADSWORTH LONGFELLOW

THE WORLD-RECORD BASS

A.J. (JUNIOR) SAMPLES became familiar to fans of the cornball television show "Hee Haw," but the mammoth comic (he weighed well over 300 pounds) got his start with the biggest fish lie in history. Junior claimed to have caught a world-record largemouth bass from Georgia's Lake Lanier, near his Cumming home. The existing record of 22 pounds, four ounces has stood since 1932—George Perry caught it in another Georgia lake, Montgomery. Junior said his was six ounces heavier.

At that time, Junior was a north Georgia hillbilly who made a semi-living running moonshine and racing stock cars. But in a 1967 radio interview, Junior's explanation of his catch was so funny that it became a best-selling record and launched him as a rural comic. It also was totally made up. The fish turned out to be a grouper—an ocean fish—and Junior probably swiped it to begin with.

Two years after the radio interview, Junior was on "Hee Haw," where he remained until his death from a heart attack in 1983. He will always remain a footnote in angling history and a fond memory for devoted fans of rustic tomfoolery.

"HE CANNOT allow the calling of Peter, James, and John from their boats to pass without a comic miraculous overdraft of fishes, with the net sinking the boats and provoking Peter to exclaim, Depart from me; for I am a sinful man, O Lord, which should probably be translated, I want no more of your miracles; natural fishing is good enough for my boats."

—GEORGE BERNARD SHAW

"I LIKE NIGHT FISHING, even though there is a molecule of terror in it. Maybe it is that tiny bit of terror that I relish, that going mano a mano with another predator in the dark. I know it is not entirely civilized, but there is nothing to compare with the sizzle of fear except, perhaps, the rush of being feared. Either condition confirms you are alive."

—PAUL QUINNETT, DARWIN'S BASS

"SHE WAS used to take delight, with her fair hand
To angle in the Nile, where the glad fish,
As if they knew who 'twas sought to deceive them,
Contended to be taken."

—PLUTARCH (DESCRIBING CLEOPATRA)

TRIALS OF FISHING

"AND I THINK, as I angle for fish,
In the hope that my hooks will attach 'em,
It's delightfully easy to fish—
But harder than blazes to catch 'em."

—WALLACE IRWIN

MUSKIE MAYHEM

MY NOSE IS RUNNING, my fingers clutching the rod handle look like purple talons, and my canoe is leaking—badly. I switch the yellow bucktail-skirted jig for a seven-inch Rapala, then adjust the electric motor's speed until my canoe is barely moving upstream. The tip of my casting rod pulses rhythmically as the plug starts working in the current.

Only a few minutes pass before the rod is nearly wrenched from my grip. Not by the hoped-for walleye, but an extremely irate 20-pound, out-of-season muskie. While I frantically try figuring out how we can best part company, it does all the wild things that make muskies the subject of angler worship. When it finally slows down, I head for shore. As the keel grates bottom, I switch off the motor and lurch stiffly to my feet. The water is only a few inches deep, so I lift my left leg over the gunwale and step cautiously onto the sloping rock shelf. I am not aware it is slippery until I lift my right foot. My left foot skids down the slanting surface while I, arms akimbo, right leg extended behind like an overweight figure skater, fight to maintain my balance. Amazingly, I get both feet under me just as the water gushes over my boot tops. I backpedal, stumble, then sit down in a foot-and-a-half of icy water. But not for long.

When the muskie is finally released it seems none the worse for wear, but my body is vibrating like a jackhammer. I turn slosh shoreward and see two old men standing on the trail. The tall, thin one speaks. I shake my head and walk closer. Through chattering teeth I say, "I'm sorry, sir, I couldn't hear you."

"I said 'I can die happy now!' Bin fishin' fer 70 years and never seen nothin' so funny."

The short, chubby fellow asks how big the muskie was. We spend a few minutes yarning about fish in general and muskie in particular. Finally, shivering so hard I can hardly speak, I say goodbye. As I leave, the tall man calls out, "Hey, young feller!" I stop and turn. "I was wonderin'—if I give you my phone number could you call next time you're comin' out." He grins. "Long as you don't charge admission, we'd like to come and watch."

"SWEET INNOCENT, the mother cried,
    And started from her nook,
    That horrid fly is put to hide
    The sharpness of the hook."

—ANN AND JANE TAYLOR,
THE LITTLE FISH THAT WOULD NOT DO AS IT WAS BID

ICE CAPADES

WITH THE EXCEPTION of a cube or two for occasional drams of medicinal scotch, I avoid ice in all forms, especially the type that covers any body of water. Past experience has convinced me that ice fishing can usually be reduced to two common denominators: hard work and terminal boredom. There is a short period of muscle-straining, sweat-inducing activity while several holes are bored, followed by long periods of total inactivity while beads of sweat turn into tiny ice crystals on one's body. The overall duration of these work/boredom periods varies in relation to the ice auger's sharpness, the augeree's lung capacity and muscle tone, and the length of time one can spend staring into a sterile hole situated over water that usually proves devoid of fish.

"**S**URF-CASTING IS calloused, hairy-chested, and big as the sea; a double-haul to a big, rising brown extrapolated to the sixth power."

—NORMAN STRUNG, FIELD & STREAM

"**A** BEAUTIFUL STREAM to one man is just so much water in which he may possibly catch so many trout."

—ARTHUR BRISBANE

"THE TEA-BLACK WATER erupts into a white fountain. The mouse disappears in a black whirlpool. I set the steel. I feel the raw energy of a big bass, its head-shaking power as it rips fly line through the pads and pulls me into a strange and wonderful place. Suddenly it is a million years ago. The stars above are the same. The lake is the same. The lava cliffs and Venus are the same. We, the bass and I, are newcomers to this ancient place. On the clock of life, we only just arrived. And yet, we found each other in the night and dark water and are now locked, predator to predator, in a struggle as old as life itself. In the black of night, on this little lake, on this little planet tucked away in the corner of the cosmos, my rod arches, my heart pounds and my hope is answered."

—PAUL QUINNETT, DARWIN'S BASS

"WHEN YOU BAIT your hook with your heart, the fish always bite!"

—JOHN BURROUGHS

LUNCHTIME GOURMET

WHEN FRANK and I went steelhead fishing, we each carried lunch in our vest. At midday we found a suitable piece of driftwood for a seat, then settled down to eat. Frank opened his bag, unwrapped a sandwich, wrinkled his nose and sighed. "Cheese," he said glumly. "God, I hate cheese." He reached back into the bag, unwrapped another sandwich, and again sighed dejectedly. "Peanut butter and jam... I hate peanut butter and jam even more."

"Why don't you ask your wife to make something you like?" I suggested.

Frank slowly shook his head. "Can't—I make my own sandwiches."

"I LOVE ANY Discourse of Rivers, and Fish and fishing..."

—IZAAK WALTON, THE COMPLEAT ANGLER

"BEWARE OF taking to collect books on angling. You will find yourself become so attached to the fascinating hobby, that you would, if necessary, pawn the shirt off your back to obtain some coveted edition."

—R.B. MARSTON

"It is just as well to remember that angling is only a recreation, not a profession. We usually find that men of the greatest experience are the most liberal and least dogmatic . . . it is often the man of limited experience who is most confident."

—Theodore Gordon

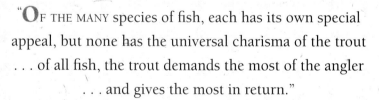

"Twas merry when
You wager'd on your angling; when your diver
Did hang a salt-fish on his hook, which he
With fervency drew up."

—William Shakespeare, Antony and Cleopatra

"Of the many species of fish, each has its own special appeal, but none has the universal charisma of the trout . . . of all fish, the trout demands the most of the angler . . . and gives the most in return."

—Joe Brooks

"The sea hath fish for every man."

—William Camden

STRUNG OUT

ROY LEARNED THE BASICS of fly-casting quickly, but had the habit of bending his wrist back too far on backcasts, causing his line to slap on the ground behind. No matter how much he concentrated, he unconsciously reverted to bending his wrist, so I retreated to the house and found a piece of heavy string. Returning to my backyard, I had him lift his forearm upright and hold the rod tip in the one o'clock position. I formed a loop around his wrist and the reel seat, then firmly knotted the string. Although able to bend his wrist forward, its rearward movement was now restricted, and his backcasts improved immediately.

About two years later I spotted Roy fishing in a mountain lake near home. He was seated in his canoe, wielding his fly rod with practiced grace and rhythm. It was not until paddling my own canoe closer that I saw a piece of string looped around his wrist and the reel seat.

"It's the same piece," he admitted. "If I don't use it, I still slap the water behind me." He grinned sheepishly and said, "Some people drink, some people smoke—I'm addicted to string."

"BEAUTY WITHOUT grace is the hook without the bait."

—RALPH WALDO EMERSON

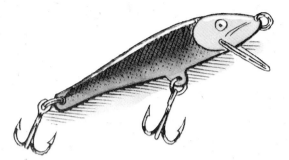

"THERE'S JOY IN the chase, over hedge and ditch flying;
'Tis pleasant to bring down the grouse on the fell;
The partridge to bag, through the low stubble trying;
The pheasant to shoot as he flies through the dell.
But what are such joys to the pleasures of straying
By the side of a stream, a long line throwing free,
The salmon and trout with a neat fly betraying?
Fit your rods, and away to the fishing with me!"

WILLIAM CHATTO

"THE SIGHT of a bonefish tail waving slowly above the
surface of the shallow water where he customarily feeds
does all kinds of things to you. You shiver and shake and
tingle all over and your mouth goes dry. It is one of the
great moments of all fishing experience."

—JOE BROOKS

THE OLD PHILOSOPHER

THE OLD MAN sat on a stump overlooking the pool, puffing on a crook-stemmed pipe. Snowy hair, face wrinkled and seamed, and a nose of truly magnificent proportions. He waved his pipe stem in salute. "Beautiful mornin'!" His voice was reedy, high-pitched.

"Indeed," I answered. "You fished her yet?"

"Yup. Fished down from the bridge."

"That's two miles!"

"Yup. Nice walk. Paid off, too." He pointed toward a nearby boulder, where a limit of cutthroat trout lay in the shade.

"Nice. That big one's a good 13 inches."

"Yup. So danged pretty I hated to keep 'em—but a man's gotta eat." He studied me over the top of his wire-rimmed spectacles. "When I was young I ran these cricks like a deer. That's how I got my nickname—Scooter. I'd scoot from one hole to another faster'n anybody. Outfished 'em all. Now I'm almost 80. I just like to visit my old fishin' holes and sit a spell. When I was young, I never stopped to look at the nice things the Almighty provided. Now it's almost too late."

The old man stood. "Well, it's nice visitin', but I gotta get goin'." He squatted by the boulder and fed the trout into his old canvas creel, then straightened and gave me a stern look. "Son, don't keep everythin' you catch. Always put back enough for seed."

As he strode swiftly away I mused about this backwoods

philosopher. A bit rough around the edges, but honest, wise and dignified. . . .

George places a mug of beer on the bar. "Well?"

"Zilch. Some real old fellow beat me to it. Had a limit of nice cutts."

His eyes narrow. "Tall skinny guy with a big nose?"

"Yeah."

"Scooter!" George spits it out. "Probably had three or four more limits stashed along the trail. He don't let nothin' go."

"You're kidding."

"No I ain't. That mealy-mouthed old crook is the worst fish hog around. Should've hung him long ago."

I study my image in the mirror behind the bar. "Pour us two shots of The Glenlivet, George."

He places two shot glasses on the bar and fills them. I pick one up. "Here's to honesty, wisdom and dignity, George—and to the world's worst judge of character."

His eyebrows raise slightly as he ponders my statement, then he smiles and touches my glass with his. "Here's lookin' at you—Your Honor."

"I AM A Brother of the Angle."

—IZAAK WALTON, THE COMPLEAT ANGLER

UNFORESEEN CIRCUMSTANCES

DESPITE OUR BEST intentions, there are times when we all encounter "unforeseen circumstances," such as when someone says:

"The store at Extremely Remote Lake sells everything you need: food, cold beer, tackle, fishing licenses, gasoline...." You arrive there to find it has changed hands and now deals exclusively in organic health food, natural fibre clothing, and anti-fishing and hunting literature.

"There are plenty of hotels and motels in town, so don't worry about reservations." You arrive to find a Shriners Convention there at precisely the same time as your planned fishing vacation.

"The old folks who own the farm don't mind the least bit if you walk through their property to the river." You arrive to discover they have sold the property to a motorcycle gang that uses several free-roaming pit bull terriers to guard their marijuana operation.

"IT SEEMS IMPOSSIBLE to exaggerate the fishing possibilities of the west coast of Florida. With a fly rod the number of fish which may be caught is purely a question of physical endurance."

—A.W. DIMOCK

"THE FIRST MEN that our Saviour dear
Did choose to wait upon Him here,
Blest fishers were; and fish the last
Food was, that He on earth did taste:
I therefore strive to follow those,
Whom He to follow Him hath chose."

—*IZAAK WALTON, THE COMPLEAT ANGLER*

"GLORY BE TO God for dappled things—
For skies as couple-color as a brinded cow;
For rose-moles all in stipple upon trout that swim."

—*GERARD MANLEY HOPKINS*

A BORING STORY

WHEN MY BUDDY Crony suggested we go ice fishing, I said firmly. "Nothing is getting me ice fishing in this weather. . . ."

"Here we are" Crony announced. "That cliff's my marker." He lined up with landmarks on either side and one on top of the cliff, then said, "Dig the first hole here. I'll get some firewood."

There was 20 inches of ice. The auger's cutters were like razors, so boring the first hole was fairly easy. The next three got progressively harder. When the cutter finally went through, I lost my balance and pitched forward, but the auger stopped my fall. Puzzled, I gave the handle a tentative crank. It ground slowly to a halt.

I staggered over to Crony and confronted him with the mud-covered cutters. "Oh, oh," he said. "That last hole must be too close to shore." He lowered his sinker into the water, testing its depth. About three feet. "Hmm . . . must've got my bearings wrong."

The two center holes were no deeper. Crony swivelled his head from side to side, searching for his elusive landmarks. "No wonder! We should have been here." Silently I handed him the auger. He, too, discovered 20 inches of ice and a foot or so of water. His next hole, much farther out, produced the same results.

I quietly munched on a mystery-meat sandwich while Crony, now red-faced and babbling incoherently, bored four more holes, ending up well over 100 yards from where I had started. They all bottomed out pretty well the same.

Despite our poor beginning, we actually made it home with a decent catch of crappie—but only by staggering back to the lodge and renting a recently vacated hut. This dismal saga does have a happy ending, though. Crony seems to have lost interest in ice fishing.

"GOD QUICKENED in the Sea and in the Rivers,
So many fishes of so many features,
That in the waters we may see all Creatures;
Even all that on the earth is to be found,
As if the world were in deep waters drowned."

—DU BARTAS, DEVINE WEEKES AND WORKES

"AS INWARD LOVE breeds outward talk,
The hound some praise, and some the hawk,
Some, better pleas'd with private sport,
Use tennis, some a mistress court:
But these delights I neither wish,
Nor envy, while I freely fish."

—WILLIAM BARRE

TIMING IS EVERYTHING

AFTER A FINE DAY of early spring steelhead fishing, it was dusk when I sloshed around the last bend. John sat on the bank, smoking a cigarette. A deep pool ran straight toward him, then veered right. As I waded knee-deep along the edge of a sloping rock shelf, John raised his hand and waved. "How'd you make out?" he asked.

Just then my foot hit a slick patch of algae and shot sideways. Still standing upright, I slid slowly down the sloping shelf, then toppled sideways and disappeared. But not for long. I promptly stood up, now in the centre of the channel, only my head and shoulders protruding from the water. "Four," I replied, reaching for my hat, which had floated off my head. "How 'bout you?"

John stared at me for a few moments, then slowly exhaled a plume of smoke. "Six."

I continued wading toward him, the water supporting my body as the slow current aided me along. I undid the suspenders on my water-filled chest waders, then John helped haul me out as they emptied and collapsed down around my legs. I sloshed soggily to my car, where I always kept a complete change of clothes. I expected John to start laughing at my performance, as I certainly would have had our roles been reversed, but he remained strangely quiet while I stripped naked, gave myself a cursory towelling, then dressed again.

During the 20-minute drive down the abandoned logging road to the highway, John hardly spoke a word, however, once the wheels hit asphalt he suddenly threw back his head and roared with loud, hysterical laughter. "Haw-aw-aw! . . . That was the funniest-looking thing I've ever seen!" he bellowed. "You-hoo-hoo looked like a submarine going down! . . . Haw-aw-aw! . . . And like 'The Creature From the Black Lagoon' coming back up."

"Well, I'm really glad I brightened up your day," I said evenly when he finally calmed down to what sounded like a terminal case of the dry heaves. "But why, pray tell, this delayed reaction?"

This triggered another wave of uncontrollable braying, then John breathed deeply to steady himself and replied, "Because now if you get mad and kick me out of the car, I can hitch-hike without having to walk all the way out to the highway." Then he started laughing again—nonstop—all the way home.

"IF YOU WISH to be happy for an hour, get intoxicated.
If you wish to be happy for three days, get married.
If you wish to be happy for eight days,
kill your pig and eat it.
If you wish to be happy forever, learn to fish."

—CHINESE PROVERB

WHISTLE WHILE YOU WADE

AFTER WATCHING a novice angler wade a fairly deep, fast-flowing stretch of river, I shook my head in wonder and said, "Pretty nice wading for a guy with limited experience. And chirping away like a canary the whole while."

"I always whistle when I'm nervous," Mark replied tersely.

"You were nervous?"

He nodded. "Extremely. Scared, really. No... terrified is more descriptive. And all I could think of was that I'd quit smoking for nothing."

"FLYCASTING, like many other things, is a matter of skill and timing—of easy rhythm rather than power. Such things can be enjoyed all through life and perhaps most of all in the more-relaxed years of age. Paddle easily. Climb slowly. Choose the right places from the experience of other days, and enjoy the view to the fullest."

—*LEE WULFF,* OUTDOOR LIFE

"A FISH, WHICH YOU can't see, deep down in the water, is a kind of symbol of peace on earth, good will to yourself. Fishing gives a man... some time to collect his thoughts and rearrange them kind of neat, in an orderly fashion. Once the bait is on the hook and the boat anchored, there's nothing to interfere with thinking except an occasional bite."

—ROBERT RUARK, THE OLD MAN AND THE BOY

"MOST ANGLERS spend their lives in making rules for trout, and trout spend theirs in breaking them."

—GEORGE ASTON

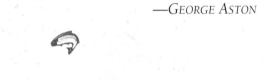

"A CERTAIN QUALITY of youth is indispensable to the successful angler, a certain unworldliness and readiness to invest yourself in an enterprise that doesn't pay in the current coin."

—JOHN BURROUGHS

THE
LIGHTER
SIDE OF
FISHING

"YOU CAN ALWAYS tell a fisherman,
but you can't tell him much."

—COREY FORD

WHAT A WONDERFUL WORM

IT IS THE BEST SINGLE LURE/BAIT that exists: the nightcrawler. Izaak Walton wrote glowingly about these superworms and wouldn't be caught without one. They are the largest of the worms used for bait since Man mated hook to something wriggly.

Of the three common fishing worms in North America (nightcrawlers, manure worms—which smell like their name implies, and the ordinary earthworm), nightcrawlers are the ultimate. They'll take bass, bluegills, catfish, or any other fish that appreciates a high-protein diet. In fact, night-crawlers are 57 percent protein, while a T-bone steak is less than 20 percent. Now I wouldn't rec-ommend a healthy diet of crawlers, but former President Jimmy Carter's cousin Hugh raises red worms for bait in Plains, Georgia, and is fond of snacking on dried worms.

Anglers argue over how to attach a nightcrawler to a hook, but most any method will work. The traditional way is to run the hook first through the collar, then a few more times through the body, leaving loops and both ends free to wriggle. This is the approved catfish baiting method, but catfish aren't picky. You can gob a nightcrawler on a No.4 hook any old way and they'll find it.

Nightcrawlers have also been known to work for pan-fish, sunfish, bullheads, lake perch, and even walleyes. And it will make fly fishermen scream, but nightcrawlers are also great for trout, especially after a rain when the water is rising and off-color.

Worm blowing may sound silly, but it works. You inject air into the poor worm to make him float off the bottom. There are commercial injectors available or you can use a hypodermic needle (although drug enforcement officials might be slow to buy the story of what you were doing with the needle). If the rhythmic bounce-bounce-bounce action of the weight stops, set the hook. You'll lose a few weights on snags, but catch a lot of fish. A bobber also keeps the bait off the bottom (Izaak Walton used one). And there are few fishing thrills more electrifying than seeing a bobber suddenly vanish with a "plunk!"

Some catch nightcrawlers for bait and electricity is one method. Stick a couple of probes in the ground, shoot the juice to them, and stand back. The "stand back" part is especially important—a mid-Missouri woman was electrocuted a few years back while probing for worms. "Must have not had it hooked up right," understated one commentator.

How to Decipher Fishing Reports

INTERPRETING WHAT FISHERMEN SAY can sometimes be as difficult as a foreign language. As a public service, here are some common translations:

"Lake Noname? Didn't you hear that it winterkilled? A guy from the fisheries branch told me that a bad avalanche took the road out last winter, so they don't plan to restock it."

This really means: "The road's a bit rough in spots, and it's absolutely crawling with big trout!"

"Bluegrouse Lake? It's been a write-off for two years now. A friend of mine tried it a couple of weeks ago and only got two little trout—and they were so muddy-tasting he couldn't eat 'em."

This really means: "There are so many big, trophy-sized fish you'll be doing them a favor by keeping a few."

"Woowoo Lake? It has some real problems—there are still lots of fish, but they're all stunted and absolutely riddled with worms."

This really means: "You dog! How did you find out about my secret lake?"

"THERE IS NO USE in your walking five miles to fish when you can depend on being just as unsuccessful near home."

—MARK TWAIN (SAMUEL LANGHORNE CLEMENS)

"WHEN FOUR FISHERMEN GET TOGETHER,
there's always a fifth."

—SPENCER APOLLONIO

"CORNED-BEEF SANDWICHES were good enough for him, but
for the catfish he'd bought at least a pound of filet steak."

—JONATHAN RABAN

"I DON'T WANT TO KETCH NO TARPON that weighs half a ton.
And feedin' clams to sheepshead isn't just what I call fun.
Of salmon when it's boiled or baked I'll say that I am fond—
But when I'm after sport I fish for pick'rel in a pond."

—NORMAN JEFFRIES

"CAN COWS TELL YOU whether or not the fish are biting?
Some folks think so. They claim that cattle graze actively
at times when the fish are hungry, and that when
cattle stop eating to rest, fish do too. So check
a pasture as you drive by."

—H.G. TAPPLY, FIELD & STREAM

BUGGED OUT

ANGLERS AND INSECTS have fought a bitter battle as old as history. I'm sure Izaak Walton battled deer flies, and before him, the angling prioress Dame Juliana Berners was tempted to call down God's wrath on some noxious insect pest. Once, out of repellant and plagued by biting midges in a fishing camp, I coated myself with guitar polish, which not only kept the midges at bay; it gave me a lovely, lustrous sheen! Technology has come a long way from the old days, though. Older repellants reacted with plastic, leaving your lures and reel handles melting in your hands.

Ticks have an uncanny knack of homing in on your most intimate spots at the most inopportune times. If you're talking to the family minister and suddenly you emit an inarticulate cry and begin to clutch yourself in a manner guaranteed to bring the vice squad, you'd better hope the good reverend is an angler. Once I darted around a stack of canned corn at the supermarket to claw at myself in blessed relief–only to find a neighbor lady shielding the eyes of her two small children as she glared at me in indignant alarm.

"Bugs," I explained.

"I'll say," she answered.

"OH THE BRAVE Fisher's life,

It is the best of any,

'Tis full of pleasure, void of strife,

And 'tis belov'd of many:

Other joys Are but toys;

Only this Lawful is,

For our skill Breeds no ill,

But content and pleasure."

—IZAAK WALTON, THE COMPLEAT ANGLER

"EVEN TO ONE AS NEW AT THE GAME AS I WAS, certain profound truths were already clear. To wit:

1. Fishing boats leak.

2. Fishing boat captains drink.

3. Any fish you lose is a marlin.

4. Fishing was always better the day before you got there.

5. Though deep-sea fishing is a very difficult sport, it can be mastered by any man or woman with average strength and inherited money."

—MAX SHULMAN, FIELD & STREAM

THE LURE OF ANGLING

FISHING PLUGS somehow became "crankbaits" in recent times, but there's nothing new about them except the name. All the so-called innovations of today's fishing lures were present a century ago—soft lures, rattle lures, you name it. But what used to be old lures, now are antiques, sometimes quite valuable. A friend of mine collects them. Is it because of the history connected with them, the stories they could tell?

"No," he says. "I just like their little faces."

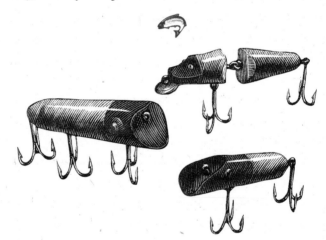

"AND ANGLING TOO, that solitary vice,
Whatever Izaak Walton sings or says:
The quaint, old, cruel coxcomb, in his gullet
Should have a hook, and a small trout to pull it."

—BYRON, DON JUAN

"THREE FISHERS WENT SAILING away to the west,
Away to the west as the sun went down;
Each thought on the woman who loved him the best,
And the children stood watching them out of the town."

—CHARLES KINGSLEY, THE THREE FISHERS

"DON'T YE TALK TO ME OF WORK!
I'm jest goin' fishin'
Where the speckled beauties lurk,
'Round the pools a-swishin'
Ne'er a thought have I of care,
Settin' on a green bank there,
Drinkin' in the soft June air,
Void of all ambition!"

—JOHN KENDRICK BANGS

"SEINE, N. A kind of net for effecting an involuntary change
of environment. For fish it is made strong and coarse, but
women are more easily taken with a singularly delicate
fabric weighted with small, cut stones."

—AMBROSE BIERCE

MOTION SICKNESS

No one knows exactly what causes seasickness. One group believes that the inner ear sends abnormal signals, causing the release of an unknown chemical that causes embarrassment and abject misery.

It is true that women are more prone to motion sickness than men and babies rarely get it (maybe because they spend so much time lying down, which pacifies their heaving inner ear; or possibly they just don't know they're supposed to be sick). However, children from two to 12 are most susceptible and it is less common after 50. Introverts are more prone than extroverts. And about half the astronauts and cosmonauts suffer from motion sickness.

You can help quell the queasies by holding your head steady or by fixing your gaze on a stationary spot, but the best remedy is: Don't think about it. Of course, that's like being waterless in the desert and convincing yourself you're not thirsty.

Toadfish may offer a remedy. Believe it or not, they have an inner ear system similar to that of the human. Scientists rock the toadfish in a high-tech cradle and monitor its brain activity. I don't know how they can interpret squiggles on a readout to mean, "Uh-oh, I'm gonna whoops!" but I'm not a scientist, just a nauseated angler.

"MONEY-GETTING MEN, men that spend all their time, first in getting, and next in anxious care to keep it; men that are condemned to be rich, and then always buy or are discontented; for these poor-rich men, we Anglers pity them perfectly, and stand in no need to borrow their thoughts to think ourselves so happy."

—*IZAAK WALTON, THE COMPLEAT ANGLER*

"THOUGH MY FLOAT goes swimmingly on,
My bad luck never seems to diminish;
It would seem that the bream
Must be scarce in the stream,
and the chub, though it's chubby, be thinnish!"

—*THOMAS HOOD*

"COMPARE THE STRONG BULL of Bashan with a saltwater smelt. Who doubts the superiority of the bull? Yet, if you drop them both into the Atlantic ocean, I will take my chances with the smelt."

—*THOMAS BRACKETT REED*

THAT'S NOT A DOGFISH

I WAS FISHING FOR TROUT and pickerel, but the only thing I ended up catching was my own dog. While switching lures, I laid a tiny cheese ball, molded around a treble hook, on the boat seat. When I checked, it was gone and Chubby, my sweet little French Brittany, was wriggling happily.

Our vet advised over the phone, "Feed him as much as possible. Surround the hook with food." (No doubt the vet was visualizing his next Caribbean cruise. He takes them; I pay for them.) Chubby wolfed my lunch and several cheeseburgers during that 100-mile trip home. He licked my ear and gazed at me with adoring eyes. My stomach rumbled, but I was too worried to eat.

We kept Chubby in the house for three days, after which the vet reported the hook had passed through the dog. I was relieved (and the vet was one giant step closer to that tropical vacation.) Chubby? He couldn't believe I was putting him back in the kennel with those other dog things.

Why, they didn't even eat cheeseburgers.

"AND WHAT WOULD BECOME of the lawyers and trout—
Trout, trout, and the devil all out,
If clients, like hoppers, warn't lyin' about—
Whack-fal-larity—whack-fal-larity—
And it warn't for wanitee? [vanity]"

—DAVID CROSS

"'RICH,' THE OLD MAN SAID DREAMILY, 'is not baying after what you can't have. Rich is having the time to do what you want to do. Rich is a little whisky to drink and some food to eat and a roof over your head and a fish pole and a boat and a gun and a dollar for a box of shells. Rich is not owing any money to anybody, and not spending what you haven't got.'"

—ROBERT RUARK, THE OLD MAN'S BOY GROWS OLDER

"ABOUT NINETY IN A HUNDRED fancy themselves anglers. About one in a hundred is an angler. About ten in a hundred throw the hatchet better than the fly."

—COL. PETER HAWKER

OBSESSION FOR FISH

Those who market the stuff call it "attractant," as if it should be worn by Christie Brinkley.

I suppose that's far better than calling it what it is: stink rowdy enough to force a dog off a gut wagon. Smear some on bait and two things are guaranteed:

1. Fish will be attracted.
2. People will be repelled.

A bottle of "fish attractant" dumped on the carpeting of your $15,000 bass boat instantly will reduce it to a $150 bass boat...and you pay them. It never will come out, no matter how much scrubbing, how many heavy rains sluice it. It will smell as virulent the day you sell the boat to an upwind buyer as it did the day you kicked it over accidentally and said, "Oh, fudge!" (or something like that). Simple stains are acceptable—marks of battle, so to speak—but stains that stink like a bucket of skunk butts are not.

Recently I opened a jar of fish attractant and distant buzzards fell to earth, wheezing and coughing. Spy satellites shifted in their orbits and the Environmental Protection Agency received thousands of reports of environmental damage. I carefully closed the jar and murmured, "I didn't want to catch fish anyway."

"THE WAITER HE TO HIM DOTH CALL,
And gently whispers—'One Fish ball.'
The waiter roars it through the hall,
'The guests they start at One Fish ball!'
The guest then says, quite ill at ease,
'A piece of bread, sir, if you please.'
The waiter roars it through the hall:
'We don't give bread with one Fish ball!'"

—*GEORGE LANE*

"IZAAK BELIEVED THAT FISH COULD HEAR; if they can, then their vocabulary must be full of strange oaths, for all anglers are not patient men."

—*IZAAK WALTON*, THE COMPLEAT ANGLER

"BUT FISH NOT, with this melancholy bait,
For this fool gudgeon, this opinion."

—*WILLIAM SHAKESPEARE*, THE MERCHANT OF VENICE

HOOKED

A FRIEND ONCE WAS FISHING with his five-year-old son when the son's lure became tangled. The helpful daddy tried to get it loose, and somehow the rear treble hook grabbed his right thumb. When he pulled away in pain, the front treble snagged his other thumb. He was miles from home, it was getting dark—and his thumbs were hooked together. "Did you ever try to drive a car with your thumbs hooked together?" he asked.

He saw lights at a rural fire department and reasoned they'd have emergency medical people. The raucous firemen were having a beer and poker party and thought this was the funniest thing they'd ever seen. While they removed the hooks, the son got to play on the fire truck and listen to the conversation.

When they got home, Junior raced into the house, shouting, "Ma! Dad got his thumbs hooked together and I got to drive a fire truck and what does @$#$!@$$#@!$ mean?"

"OF COURSE YOU STILL LOVE HER—
You love, without doubt,
But one thing above her,
And that is a trout.
It's just the old Adam,
Man back in his groove.

To quiet the madam
It's easy to prove
In the Bible you read it,
As all can perceive,
That Adam loved Eden
Before he loved Eve!"

—DOUGLAS MALLOCH

"HOW CHEERFULLY he seems to grin,
How neatly spreads his claws,
And welcomes little fishes in
With gently smiling jaws!"

—LEWIS CARROLL, ALICE'S ADVENTURES IN WONDERLAND

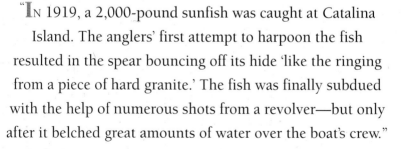

"IN 1919, a 2,000-pound sunfish was caught at Catalina Island. The anglers' first attempt to harpoon the fish resulted in the spear bouncing off its hide 'like the ringing from a piece of hard granite.' The fish was finally subdued with the help of numerous shots from a revolver—but only after it belched great amounts of water over the boat's crew."

—FIELD & STREAM

IT'S A NEW LANGUAGE

FISHING EQUIPMENT SIZE STANDARDS are as comprehensible to me as prayer in Latin. For instance, the bigger the hook, the smaller the number. A No.14 hook is much smaller than a No.8 hook. But, wait a minute—anyone could figure that system out, so they complicated it. When you get down to "1," they add a slash and a zero and then the hooks get bigger along with the numbers.

When I go in to buy a shirt, it comes in small, medium, large, and beefo (I lust for beefo, but the salesman always asks, "would you like to step over to the juniors section?"). Shirts have none of this weird jargon that infects fishing. Suppose you had to buy a "No.12" shirt, or a "2/0" pair of shorts? You just might wind up with a strangulated do-hickey!

"THAT AN IDIOT is man to believe that abstaining from flesh, and eating fish, which is so much more delicate and delicious, constitutes fasting."

—NAPOLEON I

"BAIT THE HOOK WELL; this fish will bite."

—WILLIAM SHAKESPEARE, MUCH ADO ABOUT NOTHING

"Now, who can solve my problem,
And grant my lifelong wish,
Are fishermen all big liars?
Or do only liars fish?"

—THEODORE SHARP

"WHERE THE POOLS are bright and deep,
Where the grey trout lies asleep,
Up the river and over the lea,
That's the way for Billy and me."

—JAMES HOGG

"WORMS I HATE, and never use 'em;
And, kindly friends, ne'er abuse 'em."

—J.P. WHEELDON

"SOME CIRCUMSTANTIAL EVIDENCE is very strong, as when you
find a trout in the milk."

—HENRY DAVID THOREAU

FADING IN THE STRETCH

THOSE WHO FISH SERIOUSLY for steelhead consider it a challenging and exciting pastime. However, most will also point out that it can be mystifying, demoralizing, and downright frustrating at times. Ask any knowledgeable, experienced steelheader who has worked a likely looking run diligently, yet fruitlessly, then watched an obvious neophyte blunder along behind and immediately hook a fish. It happens, but that's steelheading.

When a friend asked for advice on getting started at steelheading, I suggested some moderately-priced tackle and lures, sketched a rough map directing him to an often productive stretch of a nearby river, and left him with the advice to start off using worms. Four days later the budding steelheader excitedly related that he had followed my instructions, and on his fifth cast had hooked and landed a mint-bright steelhead weighing 19 pounds. At the time, despite having caught hundreds of steelhead, my personal best was 17 pounds.

"Pity," I said.

He looked puzzled. "Why do you say that?"

"Getting your 'glory fish' so soon. You'll probably never get another steelhead that big if you fish till you're 90."

Joe kept haunting that river, but after paving its bottom with lead sinkers, hooks, and swivels, he had nothing to show for his effort except ruddy cheeks and chilblains. He spent the remainder of the season traveling to more Vancouver Island streams than I previously knew existed, but ended the season with only that first steelhead to his credit. He took up golf the following spring. Maybe Joe quit steelheading too soon, but maybe not—he is considered an excellent golfer.

"Enjoy the stream, O harmless fish;
and when an angler for his dish,
Through gluttony's vile sin,
Attempts, a wretch, to pull thee out,
God give thee strength, O gentle trout,
To pull the raskall in!"

—John Wolcot

"The charm of fishing is that it is the pursuit of what is elusive but attainable, a perpetual series of occasions for hope."

—John Buchan

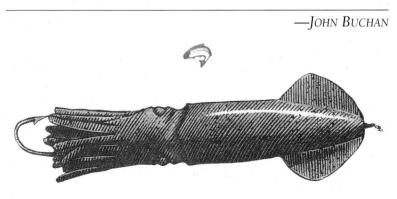

HOOKS,
LINES
& SINKERS

"COME LIVE WITH ME, and be my love,
And we will some new pleasures prove
Of golden sands, and crystal brooks,
With silken lines and silver hooks.

—JOHN DONNE, THE BAIT

SOMETHING OLD AND SOMETHING OLDER

WINTER STEELHEADERS ARE, without doubt, one of the strangest critters on this great planet. On days when temperatures hover around freezing and sane people huddle near warm stoves, winter steelheaders wade waist-deep into icy rivers, then stand there as happy as if they are in their right minds. They outdo even fly-fishers when it comes to strange behavior and idiosyncrasies, saddle themselves with self-imposed restrictions regarding tackle and bait, and decree how they should or shouldn't fish.

One of the most disconcerting traits of winter steelheaders is how they totally ignore modern progress. Each year the fishing tackle industry spends millions of dollars researching, designing, manufacturing, and advertising reels that are "All new!" and "Improved!" Spinning reels have sprouted multi-disc drag systems, automatic bails, and supersonic-retrieve ratios; casting reels are free-spooled, level-winding, comput-erized, and direct-drive—and some might soon offer a choice of an automatic transmission or four on the floor. Do winter steelheaders care? Not a bit. While anglers elsewhere eagerly snap up these wonders at prices ranging up to $300, stodgy steelheaders insist on using single-action, center-pin casting reels of a design that originated over 300 years ago.

They are totally devoid of frills, bells, and whistles, but steelheaders gladly pay similar amounts for these simple line winches. Not only that, some eagerly pay more than double those amounts for handmade reels, then happily go on waiting lists for up to a year or more for the privilege of forking over their money.

If you happen to have any extremely old center-pin reels laying around your basement or garage, you may well have the makings of a small fortune. Should steelheaders hear you possess an ancient Silex, Major, or Jewel from The House of Hardy, they will flock to your door waving fistfuls of money. The older the better. No, they don't want them for display purposes; they intend to use them. Thus, if you come across an old Atlantic salmon rod fashioned from greenheart, ironwood, or tubular steel, or some catgut leaders and a hank of braided horsehair line, mention it to any friends who fish for winter steelhead. They are always interested in using something "new" in ancient relics while pursuing their favorite sport.

"FISH SAY, they have their stream and pond;
But is there anything beyond?"

—*RUPERT BROOKE*, HEAVEN

THE PERFECT FLY

THERE IS A SENSE OF PRIDE in creating a fly with everything as it should be: tail cocked just so, wings perfectly mounted, hackle precisely the right length. These rare wonders I set aside and give to friends; the others go into my fly box. They might be a touch deformed, their wings a bit cockeyed, or tails twisted a bit to one side. The important thing is they catch fish.

I have yet to see a trout or bass inspect a fly with a magnifying glass to see whether its head was finished with a series of half hitches or whipped; or use calipers to check a tail's length; or if the blue dun hackle was from a genuine Andalusian cock or merely dyed. Using my less-than-perfect flies is something like driving a brand new car with a big dent in one fender—they don't look quite as nice, but still get the job done.

"ANGLERS ARE TOO APT to pin their faith to two or three favorite flies, and to imagine that if the trout should not rise at these, they will not take at all."

—THEODORE GORDON

"GOLDENROD GRUBS make excellent bait for winter bluegill fishing. After the first frost, look for stalks with balloon-like

bulges and collect them in bundles for storage in the
garage or cellar. When you need bait, slice open a
swelling and extract the grub."

—*H.G. Tapply, Field & Stream*

"The contentment which fills the mind of the angler
at the close of his day's sport is one of the
chiefest charms in his life."

—*William Cowper Prime*

"But should you lure
From his dark haunt beneath the tangled roots
Of pendent trees the monarch of the brook,
Behoves you then to ply your finest art."

—*James Thomson, The Seasons*

"Our disputants put me in mind of the skuttle fish, that
when he is unable to extricate himself, blackens all the water
about him, till he becomes invisible."

—*Joseph Addison*

A CASE OF SELF-ABUSE

I CAN DO WITHOUT ICE FISHING. Really. I find no pleasure in freezing assorted extremities and necessary body parts while crouched beside an unproductive hole drilled—always at great physical effort—through a thick layer of frozen water. Ice huts are out. Most of my friends are terminally addicted to tobacco—which makes incarceration in one for more than ten seconds a test of respiratory endurance. However, despite my aversion to ice fishing I frequently find myself—always against my better judgment—trudging the arctic wastes of various lakes.

On one such trip, Larry caught the first fish, a 14-inch, hatchery-raised lake trout. My minnow-baited hook was taken moments later. A spectacular battle lasting all of five seconds ensued. Frigid, 14-inch lake trout are not exactly world famous for strength and endurance.

Time passes slowly in winter-chilled air, even more so when the fish refuse to cooperate. The sun was directly overhead and we had bored several more holes before my companion hooked his second laker. By which time, so many sticks marked our barren holes the lake looked like a miniature dead forest. We finally quit at mid-afternoon with three fish apiece, and started back to the car.

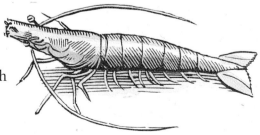

Larry made the return trip in 20 minutes; I took nearly an hour. My somewhat lighter friend walked over the partially thawed crust of snow, but I broke through with every step. Not immediately—only after lifting myself up out of each previous hole just long enough to put full weight on my foot. I finally arrived at the car, my trail marked by a ragged line of water-blackened holes. My boots had long since filled, and my voice was hoarse from describing winters in general, ice fishing in particular, and Larry's questionable ancestry.

He was seated in the car, poring intently over a map and making notations on the border. "You know," he said, "if the ice holds out we can fish a different lake every weekend for the next ten weeks."

If you think grown men don't cry, I am here to tell you we all have our limit.

"...HE THAT VIEWS THE ANCIENT Ecclesiastical Canons... shall find Angling allowed to clergymen as being a harmless recreation, a recreation that invites them to contemplation and quietness."

—IZAAK WALTON, THE COMPLEAT ANGLER

FORGETTING THE IMPORTANT PART

SOMETIMES ANGLERS FORGET to finish a statement, which can lead to interesting times if you follow their advice. Say your informant states, "There won't be any mosquitoes this time of the year," *forgetting to add:* "The blackflies kill them off."

"There aren't any grizzlies or black bears in that entire area," *forgetting to add:* "They're afraid of the rattlesnakes."

"The road up is a bit steep in spots, but you won't have any problem," *forgetting to add:* "As long as your four-wheel drive vehicle has a good winch."

"You won't need tire chains," *forgetting to add:* "If you happen to be driving a vehicle with Caterpillar tracks."

"There was a slide near the top of Bottomless Gulch, so the road's a bit narrow, but you can make it through okay," *forgetting to add:* "If you are riding a mountain bike."

"From where you park, it's only a half mile to the lake," *forgetting to add:* "Up a vertical mountain face that was recently clear-cut and burnt over."

"A RODLESS WALTON of the brooks,
A bloodless sportsman, I."

—*SAM WALTER FOSS*, THE BLOODLESS SPORTSMAN

"Should a 5-pounder explode on my popper right now, and if I can set the hook, it will be a fight so fundamental and so wild and natural and instinctive that, for the duration of the battle, I might as well be the bass."

—Paul Quinnett, Darwin's Bass

"He seems to regard angling as an amusement in which to pass the time pleasantly, rather than as a craft to be closely studied."

—W. Earl Hodgson

"The world has no better fish than the bass of Otsego [a lake whitefish]; it unites the richness of the shad to the firmness of the salmon."

—James Fenimore Cooper

"Men lived like fishes; the great ones devour'd the small."

—Algernon Sidney

GOOD LUCK

YEARS AGO, steelhead anglers fishing one central Vancouver Island river gave one riverbank farm a very prudent wide berth out of respect for the bad-tempered Doberman pinscher residing there. The standard procedure was to wade the river well up or downstream from either boundary of the farm, then proceed along the opposite bank. Quite often the big dog matched the progress of an angler with his own stiff-legged gait, teeth bared and hackles bristling. Once the fence marking the end of his territory was reached, the beast would stand guard until the interloper was well out of sight.

One winter day while struggling into my chest waders, a middle-aged friend trudged slowly up the trail toward me. Obviously distressed, he was breathing hard and sweat glistened on his flushed face. Concerned, I asked, "Are you okay, Bob?"

"Yeah," he replied, "but it's a good thing I haven't got a weak heart."

"What happened?"

He propped his long spinning rod against my car and fumbled with trembling hands through the pockets of his fishing vest for his pipe and tobacco pouch. "You know that big fir layin' across the trail downstream?"

I nodded. Anyone using the trail had the option of crawling over the long-dead forest giant, or walking around it. As it was about four feet in diameter where it crossed the trail, most of us chose to go over by leaning our rod against the trunk, scrambling up one side, then sliding down the other.

"Well," Bob continued, "I crawled up on top and sat there for a moment, then I swung my legs around and started to slide down—and saw this big patch of black hair moving right under my feet. I let out a yell and almost gave myself a hernia trying to claw my way back on top of the log, but down I went—right on top of it. God! All I could think about was those long teeth going for my throat."

I was incredulous. "Do you mean to tell me you fell on top of that dog and he didn't tear you apart?"

"It wasn't the Doberman, thank God," Bob replied, his voice expressing relief. "It was only a bear."

"I YIELD TO NO ONE in love and admiration for the brook trout. I was perfectly familiar with it before I ever saw a black bass; but I am not so blinded by prejudice but that I can share that love with the black bass, which for several reasons is destined to become the favorite game-fish of America."

—JAMES HENSHALL

LETTING GO

IT TOOK ONLY THREE MUSKIES to discover I have no desire whatsoever to hang one of those monsters on my wall. Of any size. Even that magical 70-pounder that will appear some day to topple all existing records. I have no argument with people who fish for trophies, or with those who have mounted fish on their walls. Many are fine works of art executed by skilled artists—I simply don't want one.

I have found that releasing muskies is a state of mind, and you should program yourself to do it as often as possible. If you have a need to keep one, fine. But after you have a trophy or two hung on the wall, and after you discover walleye, pike, and smallmouth bass all taste a lot better, maybe you'll start examining your "needs."

The best way to start is to set a goal: a 20-pounder, perhaps (or 30 or 40), then start releasing all fish that fall short. I can guarantee that when you watch that first legal-sized muskie swim away, you will feel a sense of pride and accomplishment that far outshines anything that comes from holding up a dead fish for a few admiring glances that are quickly forgotten. And believe me, as your number of released fish grows, so will your sense of achievement.

"WHO HEARS the fishes when they cry?"

—HENRY DAVID THOREAU

"IN A BOWL TO SEA went wise men three,
On a brilliant night in June:
They carried a net, and their hearts were set
On fishing up the moon."

—*THOMAS LOVE PEACOCK*, THE WISE MEN OF GOTHAM

"BUT AS FOR YOU, that will tarry, and worship the Lord Jesus Christ this Day, I will pray unto Him for you, that you may take Fish till you are weary."

—*COTTON MATHER*

"(SECOND FISHERMAN): HELP, master, help! Here's a fish hangs in the net, like a poor man's right in the law; 'twill hardly come out."

—*WILLIAM SHAKESPEARE*, PERICLES, PRINCE OF TYRE

"THE CARP IS THE QUEEN OF RIVERS: a stately, a good, and a very subtil fish…"

—*IZAAK WALTON*, THE COMPLEAT ANGLER

POP QUIZ

ANY EXPERIENCED ANGLER should have no problem determining the true meaning of the following statements:

"Don't bother with rain gear—it's always sunny during July and August."

"That salmon run shows up on the same day every year, just like clockwork."

"No sense in going too early, no one ever fishes there."

"They always have plenty of boats to rent."

"This canoe doesn't leak, so you won't need a bailing can."

Finally, a passing grade if you can determine the true meaning of this most commonly heard statement: "I know a shortcut...."

"WHILE FLOWING RIVERS yield a blameless sport
Shall live the name of Walton: Sage benign!
Whose pen, the mysteries of rod and line
Unfolding, did not fruitlessly exhort."

—WILLIAM WORDSWORTH

"I CAME FROM A RACE OF FISHERS; trout streams
gurgled about the roots of my family tree."

—JOHN BURROUGHS

"A FIDDLER ON A FISH through waves advanced,
He twang'd the catgut, and the dolphins danced."

—ARION

"THERE IS NOT A PLEASANTER SUMMER DAY'S amusement than a
merry cruise after the Blue-Fish, no pleasanter close to it
than the clam-bake, the chowder, and the broiled Blue-Fish,
lubricated with champagne."

—FRANK FORRESTER

APPEARANCES CAN BE . . .

MY BUDDY RALPH lives and works in the city, but spends weekends and holidays at his lakeside cabin. One time, while he was wielding his fly rod with particular skill along the rocky shoreline, I readied my camera from a distance, hoping to photograph him fighting fish—despite the fact that the confirmed bachelor dresses like a tramp while at his cabin, and never shaves.

While he was methodically prospecting each potential location I detected an unusual sound for that small lake: a high-powered outboard motor. It grew louder, then a wide-bodied boat towing a water skier curved around the point and headed straight toward Ralph's canoe. I feared the driver didn't see him, but it finally veered sharply away. As they  roared past, the driver and two occupants shouted and raised cans of beer in mock salute. The skier, leaning almost parallel to the water, skittered within 20 feet of the canoe, the lacy curtain of water from his skis arcing high into the air and totally drenching Ralph. Moments later the boat's wake arrived, almost capsizing him.

As the boat disappeared around another point, Ralph reeled in, then paddled toward his cabin. I walked back to my van. By the time I arrived at Ralph's he had changed into dry clothes, and was buttoning his shirt.

"Hope you dried behind your ears," I said by way of greeting.

"Yep. I saw you up on the bluff. Spying on me, eh?"

"Nope—taking photographs."

"That right? And what did you photograph?"

"A motor-drive sequence. Ten shots of them buzzing your canoe, and the water skier giving you a bath—which they probably thought you really needed."

"Very funny." Ralph scratched the greying stubble on his chin, then picked up his electric shaver. "Which lens were you using?"

"Two hundred."

"Hmm . . . strong enough to read the registration number?"

"Even the brand of beer they were drinking."

Ralph smiled. "Any chance of seeing them when you get the film developed?"

"No problem."

He finished shaving, then said he was leaving to start a string of evening shifts in town but would stop by the resort—which has the lake's only boat launching ramp. Ralph locked his cabin and we strolled to our vehicles.

As he drove off I sat for awhile, musing over the difference a shave and the sharply-pressed police sergeant's uniform made in my friend's appearance.

"**H**E SHINES AND STINKS like rotten mackeral by moonlight."

—*JOHN RANDOLPH*

"**T**HE DAY WAS FINE—not another hook in the brook."

—*DANIEL WEBSTER*

"**O**UR PLENTEOUS STREAMS a various race supply;
The bright-ey'd perch, with fins of Tyrian dye,
The silver eel, in shining volumes roll'd,
The yellow carp, in scales bedrop'd with gold,
Swift trouts, diversify'd with crimson stains,
And pykes, the tyrants of the wat'ry plains."

—*ALEXANDER POPE*

"WE HAVE other fish to fry."

—*RABELAIS*, WORKS

"'TIS BLITHE the mimic fly to lead,
When to the hook the salmon springs
And the line whistles through the rings."

—SIR WALTER SCOTT

"WHEN I GET UP at five in the morning to go fishing, I wake
my wife up and ask, 'What'll it be, dear, sex or fishing?'
And she says, 'Don't forget your waders.'"

—*PAUL QUINNETT*, DARWIN'S BASS

"HOW LIKE FISH we are: ready, nay eager, to seize upon
whatever new thing some wind of circumstance shakes
down upon the river of time! And how we rue our haste,
finding the gilded morsel to contain a hook."

—*ALDO LEOPOLD*, A SAND COUNTY ALMANAC

FISHY FACTS

"COME WARM WEATHER, I'm going to take a
kid fishing; I hope you do too. But nothing
would make me happier than to look
across the cove or down the stream and see
a young one help an old one remember
what it was like to be young in Springtime."

—GENE HILL, FIELD & STREAM

No Respect

Isaak Walton called it "The Queen of the River." Trout? Salmon? Not hardly. Walton, in company with many European anglers, was in love with the carp. American anglers always have scorned the carp (although it originally was stocked in this country by enthusiasts who thought it would be the food and sport fish of the future).

The times are a-changin', though. There is an active Carp Anglers Group, located in Illinois, which began in 1993 as a newsletter with a circulation of 30. Today, nearly 500 members proudly claim membership and there have been two national meetings, the first of which was associated with the Chicago Carp Classic. The Chicago River, long not much more than an open sewer for the Windy City, has been cleaned up. It is now "a tremendous venue for carp," in the words of the CAG. Carp anglers caught more than one thousand pounds of carp during the second annual meeting in 1995, including a 22-pound trophy caught by Bernie Haines (who was named the Chicago Carp King, as well as North American Carp Champion).

Today's carp anglers realize that, like it or not, we're stuck with the burly fish that has been around for more than 100 years...and we'd better learn to enjoy it.

Mark Anthony, engaged in a fishing contest with Cleopatra from her barge, was the first (but hardly the last) to cheat in a fishing contest. He hired divers to put fish on his hook. Cleopatra topped this the next day when her divers put dried fish on his hooks.

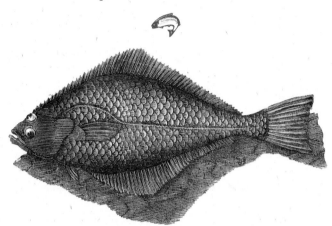

COLONEL PUREFOY FITZGERALD caught a 40-pound pike in 1865 after it hit the floating head of a croquet mallet tossed into the lake by his three-year-old son.

CATFISH USE BARBELS to smell and fondle baits. They take worms or minnows faster than unusual baits, so wait longer than usual before you move your bait and you catch more fish.

ONE LESS BACKCAST per cast should mean 10% to 20% more fish in a day.

ERNEST HEMMINGWAY caught the first two tuna brought whole into Bimini off his famous boat the *Pilar.* At times he used a Tommygun to keep sharks away from his catches.

THE OLDEST RECORD in the books is Dr. C. C. Abbot's 4-pound, 3-ounce yellow perch, set in 1864.

IN 1801, the Reverend W. B. Daniel, in his book *Rural Sports,* suggested readers fish for pike by using a minnow baited line tied to a goose's foot.

"NEEDLE THREADERS" from the sewing shop help those with older eyes, or larger fingers, get a 4X leader through that No. 16 fly's eye.

PARMIS' EPITAPH from the third century B.C. says he had a fish in his mouth while changing his lure. The fish's dying convulsions carried it down his throat and Parmis choked to death.

JAPANESE BUDDHISTS believe that fish can be eaten without sin, while animals can't. It's worth noting that, unlike

Europeans, Japanese categorized whales and porpoises as "fish." A few even called deer "mountain whales."

IN 1960, Fidel Castro won the Hemingway Tournament out of San Francisco do Paula, Cuba, with three marlin.

THE PARTRIDGE HOOK COMPANY offered a two-eyed hook one year for Teacher and Student dual control casting. Their "long line release" hook bends straight with a jerk, but transmutes into a standard hook if you boil it in salted water. Note: These releases came out April 1.

FISHING CLERICS started with St. Peter, but the Reverend Robert Nobbes wrote *The Complete Troller* in 1682. It covered trolling for pike.

KELLEY EVERETTE'S PACIFIC BLUE MARLIN remains the outstanding record of all time. The 1,103½-pound fish was taken on a 30-pound test line. (That's 37 times the line test!) And Kelley did this with a reattached right hand and a leg lost to an Alaskan Pipeline accident.

SAY UNCLE

BACK IN 1920, Alan Jones and Urban Schreiner were fishing in Wisconsin. They preferred to use live frogs, but it was dry and frogs were scarce. So Jones and Schreiner went to a local butcher shop, bought a chunk of pork fat with rind on it and carved some frog imitations. Thus was born the Uncle Josh pork frog, a legendary fishing lure, which hit the market in 1922.

And who was Uncle Josh? He was a cornball rural comedian, popular on the scratchy phonograph records of the day. The two anglers liked Uncle Josh (though if you ever hear one of his recordings it's difficult to understand why) and they named their new bait in his honor.

Today, Uncle Josh's catalog has a contented-looking pig on the front, with dotted lines showing the body areas that are associated with various Uncle Josh baits. This is probably an advertising gimmick, but the original pork frog allegedly comes from the belly. The pork crawdad is a ham product, while the pork shoulder produces Twin Tails and Bass Strips.

Yes, one might say (if one has the courage) that after 75 years, Uncle Josh still is bringing home the bacon.

IN CASES where "no fishing" zones below dams prohibit access some anglers use radio controlled boats to carry large plugs up to the dam face. The plug is jerked free and retrieved.

EACH LURE has an optimum speed range. So hum varied tunes and keep time as you reel. Some days Mozart may produce; other days it's Country Joe and the Fish tempos.

THINK "GLOW-IN-THE-DARK" floats are new? Robert Howlett's *Angler's Sure Guide of 1706* offers up translucent quill floats stuffed with glow-worms!

SOME FRESHWATER FISH, like perch, have golden eyes that are red-biased so the golden color prevents blue from hitting the retina. Hence a reason for red lure effectiveness.

ORDER IN THE COURT

IN 1960, a Missouri court gave a ruling that today might bring joy to a fisherman but would make woman's rights advocates foam at the mouth. Lowell asked for a divorce from Minnie because of "indignities." He said she interfered with his fishing, hunting, and trading livestock.

The court said, "We will agree with respondent in his definition of Stone County freedoms that a husband has a RIGHT to go fishing. And we will go further and say that this RIGHT extends to fishing without the constant and ever-present impediment of female presence and participation, if such be against the will of the husband.

"It is a wise wife who accords her husband that freedom—in moderation—and a foolish wife who interferes," the judges said. But they refused to give Lowell his freedom, saying, "The studied, constant, and repeated interference with that right over a long period of time could be, under certain conditions, an indignity, but two or three or four isolated instances of insistence upon going along, or insistence upon his not going (either fishing or turkey shooting) over a period of six years do not, in and of themselves, constitute a constant and studied course of conduct amounting to indignities which render life intolerable."

Then the judges couldn't help adding, "To use a Southern Missouri expression, she wanted to tie the stake rope a little too short."

THERE'S A EUROPEAN CATFISH called "the wels," which reportedly runs to 15 feet and more than 675 pounds. Some German duck hunters report retrievers gobbled by these critters.

YOU CAN RAPIDLY CLEAR a fish camp of Yellow Jackets (wasps) by suspending a piece of raw bacon or fish over a pan full of water with a little detergent added to eliminate surface tension. Save the drowned wasps; spoon them into a stream to create a hatch, and use a patter like a McGinty to take some big trout.

MOST EUROPEAN FISHING EXPERTS claim that carp in heavily pressured areas are far smarter than bass or trout.

HALIBUT SAVE THEIR FIGHT for the boat. To stun one quickly, whomp it on the small of the tail—not the head.

PRIOR TO THE CUBAN REVOLUTION, Ted Williams—the last baseball player to hit .400—used to fish the flats around the Isle of Pines, Cuba, for bonefish.

SHOALS OF TUNA swim in a parabolic curve so that any fish that swims away from the tuna at right angles becomes another tuna's "dinner guest." It's thought this is done by a combination of scent and lateral line pressure sensors.

IN THE 18TH CENTURY, an American privateer skipper tossed his letters of marque over the side when approached by a British warship, but he was later hanged to death when sailors on the warship caught a shark with the letters in its belly.

FISH BITE BETTER just before a rain because low air pressure makes fish food on the bottom rise.

A FISHERMAN IN ZANZIBAR once caught a butterflyfish, the markings of which in Arabic said "There is no God but Allah" on one side and "A warning from Allah" on the other. Unfortunately, the fellow could not read and sold this "million dollar" fish for pennies.

JUST AFTER A BIG STORM, the downwind side of lakes becomes productive as gamefish cruise in to harvest minnows, crayfish, and other bait killed by "storm surf."

IN 1932, GEORGE PERRY set his 22-pound, 4-ounce largemouth bass record with a $1.35 lure, fished with a shared rod and reel that cost $1.33 from a boat built with 75 cents worth of lumber scraps.

THE WONDERFUL RAINBOW TROUT in New Zealand came, along with Valley Quail, from California when smolts were netted from the Russian River just north of San Francisco.

A PURELY DEVILISH LURE

SOME OF THE MOST POPULAR FISHING LURES have peculiar
naming histories. The best-known lure-naming story is that
of the Dardevle, a red-and-white spoon which originally
was called the Daredevil. But because of fears that religious
types would object to the association of the Devil with a
fishing lure, the spelling was changed. This sensitivity is
somewhat dampened when you look at the lure and see a
grinning red fellow with horns and a trident as the lure
logo. For the record, the Dardevle originally celebrated the
U.S. Marines of World War I, who were nicknamed the Dare
Devils by their Allies. Luremaker Lou Eppinger's concern
for the religious sensibilities of his buyers wasn't shared by
other manufacturers who named the Devil Horse and the
Hell Diver.

GRAYLING GET THEIR SCIENTIFIC NAME, *Thymallus*, because
they are supposed to smell like thyme when fresh-caught.

FLY FISHERS STARTED "cheating" on floating flies by using
cork bodies as far back as 1590.

FINS TIP OFF FISH BEHAVIOR. Big fins and fat bodies mean
sudden stops and starts and ambush feeding, like bass.

Long bodies with big fins mean cruising with sudden darts to feed, like trout. High-speed fish have small fins and use the body and tail for sustained speeds.

Largemouth black bass may eat some odd things. A "record" fish was submitted to the California Department of Fish and Game with a 2½-pound diver's weight in its stomach.

A 39-pound pike was found in a British haystack next to a pond, with its mouth tightly clamped to the severed tip of a fox tail. Did the pike bite the tail tip and get dragged up on the bank?

More Fish Tales

Wildlife rumors usually are about a fish big enough to swallow automobiles. A persistent one is that huge catfish have clamped down on some unfortunate's arm and drowned him. No one ever has seen it, but many know someone who knew someone whose cousin was there when it happened. A Missouri conservation agent once used a rumor to cool a rash of illegal fishing. He mentioned at the coffee shop that the conservation department was stocking alligators. "Sure was quiet on the river for a while," the agent said.

Kentucky allegedly has striped bass at Lake Cumberland big enough to snack on coonhounds careless enough to try for a drink of water at the lake's edge. Hawaii has its Wahiawa Monster. Two beer-drinking anglers in a 14-foot boat stringered a large bass. They fell asleep and were awakened by a commotion and saw the "monster," its head beyond the bow of the boat, tail beyond the stern. The bass had been partly filleted. They reported a sea monster had attacked their trophy bass. One theory is that the "monster" was two pongee, a large fish, engaged in spawning behavior, and that the stringered bass had been filleted by a mongoose. "But the anglers got many free dinners and much publicity," says William Devick of the Hawaii conservation department. Who would have thought fish stories could be so profitable?

DURING WINTER, yellow perch seem to be the most civilized fish, with peak bite periods in mid-morning and mid-afternoon.

ICE ANGLERS should take along a piece of plywood big enough for their feet. This keeps your feet off the ice (and that means warmer toes). When a fish slips off the hook, kick the plywood over the augered hole and retrieve your catch at your leisure.

CATCH AND RELEASE STATISTICS vary. It's suggested at least five percent of fish taken on artificial lures and flies die. (So "100 trout catch and release days" may not be as bloodless as some might think.)

IN 1765, A 28-POUND PIKE was caught in the Ouse River with the watch of a recently drowned man in its stomach.

SALMON AND TROUT use a body "C-bend" to generate forces that allow leaps and jumps. Later in their life, fish use a body "S-bend" to dash at bait.

ICE AGE CAVE DWELLERS in Southern France left carvings of what appear to be salmon or sea trout on reindeer horn.

THE WORLD-RECORD STEELHEAD was so big that it was weighed in as a salmon in a Bell Island Fishing Contest–by an Alaskan Fish and Game Biologist! How big? Eight-year-old David White set his record of 42 pounds, 2 ounces in 1970.

IF YOU CAN'T READ THE SPIFFY "fishing" thermometers, check out your photo shop for chemical thermometers with large, easy-to-read dials.

To IMPROVE YOUR CASTING ACCURACY from boat to bank, simply keep your distance from shore constant. This lets you replicate the motion each time.

IN GERMANY IN 1806, a hailstone the size of a hen's egg held a small carp that was swept into the clouds by a waterspout and frozen.

WHEN SMOKE from chimneys rises straight in the air, fishing should be good because of high air pressure.

TODAY'S WADERS SHOULD COUNT THEIR BLESSINGS when they note the following Victorian advice: "never to wade above the fifth button on one's waistcoat" and "to check their legs when fishing cold water and return home if the legs turn purple or black."

THE REASON BROOK TROUT seem so stunted in Western waters relates to the planting of brook trout stocks captured from Adirondack streams, where little trout mature in two years. The much bigger Canadian brook trout mature much later.

THE NAME GAME

IF YOU HAPPEN TO BE FISHING for black bass, be advised: They aren't bass. In fact, they really are sunfish. And many anglers generically call all sunfish, except bass, "perch." But they aren't perch. Perch are a big family, but they don't include any of the sunfishes. Rather, they include walleye (which some anglers call "jack salmon," though they aren't salmon), and darters. Confused? It gets worse.

Most anglers don't know that "bass" and crappies are in the same family, but "bass" and bass aren't. Not real bass, anyway—such critters as striped, white, and yellow bass. "The sea basses are sometimes referred to as the 'true' basses to distinguish them from the smallmouth bass, spotted bass, largemouth bass, and rock bass, which are all members of the sunfish family," says Bill Pflieger, who wrote the book on Missouri fishes.

This confusion over fish names is why taxonomists use Latin. As sure as you give a fish a common name, someone comes along and calls a bowfin a "cypress trout." A bowfin (also a dogfish, grinnel, grindle, and mudfish) at least has only itself to take care of—it is the only member of its family in the United States.

And, considering what a bowfin looks like, that is a blessing.

Cᴏʙᴡᴇʙꜱ ᴏʀ ᴅᴇᴡ on the grass in the morning signals a good fishing day.

Oɴᴇ ᴏꜰ ᴛʜᴇ ᴍᴏꜱᴛ ᴇʟᴜꜱɪᴠᴇ ʀᴇᴄᴏʀᴅꜱ of all time is an M. Salazar's 283-pound Tarpon taken on Lake Maracaibo, Venezuela, on March 19, 1956. Neither photos nor details of the event are available.

Tᴏ ʀᴇᴍᴏᴠᴇ ᴏᴅᴏʀ, wash your hands with a bit of toothpaste after you clean fish; rub toothpaste on dull metal spoons and spinners and they shine right up.

Fᴇᴍᴀʟᴇ ʙʀᴏᴏᴋ ᴛʀᴏᴜᴛ have smaller heads than males.

Tʜᴇ ꜰᴀᴍᴏᴜꜱ *Ompax spatuloides* fish species from Australia has only one member, which later turned out to be made from the bill of a platypus, the head of a lungfish, the body of a mullet, and the tail of an eel. Queensland comics concocted the creature to put on the Director of the Brisbane Museum.

HEY, WHO ATE THE BAIT?

THERE ARE FEW FISH BAITS that not only are highly palatable to fish, but also to man. The crayfish is one. The word "crayfish" came from the German "Krebiz" or crab. (Actually, you can call them crayfish, crawdads, or crawfish.) And it's not a fish, but rather a freshwater lobster.

There are two edible parts of a crawdad—its muscular tail, which is far more subtle in taste than shrimp but equivalent in size, and its "fat" or liver, a yellow glop that is the preferred lubricant to butter or margarine in most Cajun crawfish dishes. The crawdad is distributed worldwide (some 500 species, of which 350 exist in North America, including one that measures a whopping eight inches from claw tip to tail).

A sizable chunk of the artificial lure world is imitative of crawdads: jigs, various crankbaits, some flies, and pork or other soft-bodied lures. Research shows that about 70 percent of a spotted bass's diet is crawdads. Smallmouth bass are equally fond of them. Crawdads dangling from a trotline are guaranteed to waylay passing catfish; and trout love crawfish. The ideal bait crawdad is about two inches long, tail to toenail, and soft-shelled. For people, the individual serving is 3 to 4 pounds. Eating-size crawdads run 8 to 12 per pound and a four-pound serving yields about a half-pound of edible meat.

For hungry anglers, though, the hardest choice might be whether to use a crawdad for bait . . . or eat it themselves.

WHAT FISH HAS THREE EYES, one nostril, and two-thirds of a pair of eyes, and as a youngster sees with its tail? Give up? It's a lamprey! They are direct descendants of the earliest fishes that appeared more than 400 million years ago.

WADERS LAST LONGER if you don't hang them in the garage, attic, or other places where they get very hot and very cold. Coat clear silicone bathroom caulk on seams and other stressed spots to increase wear.

LETTIE ROBINSON CAUGHT A SIX-POUND black crappie from a seaplane canal back in 1969. Howard Rogillio, still at the Louisiana Fisheries Department, weighed the fish, but it isn't a record because Louisiana had only one record for both white and black crappies.

THE ROOT NAME OF "TROUT" goes back to an ancient Germanic root "trauz," which means "to bite."

FISH SEEM TO HAVE A 10 TO 12 BODY LENGTHS per second speed limit. Tuna might make 20 lengths per second. So big fish can usually swim faster than small fish.

IN CEYLON, NOW SRI LANKA, *Hook silver*—symbolic fish hooks made from silver—was legal currency.

PADDLEFISH, one of the most primitive fishes in North America, can live 30 years and top 200 pounds in the Mississippi River System and Mobile Bay drainage.

WAHOO ARE THE LARGEST MEMBERS of the mackerel family.

WALTER MAXWELL'S tiger shark weighed in at 1,780 pounds after reportedly losing more than 10 percent of its body weight. As a "grander" (over 1,000 pounds), it may be the largest fish ever taken from the shore.
And Maxwell caught it off a pier!